W9-AES-026

SHAKESPEARE & JONSON

THEIR REPUTATIONS IN THE
SEVENTEENTH CENTURY COMPARED

*

GERALD EADES
BENTLEY

UNIVERSITY OF CHICAGO PRESS · CHICAGO

822.33
XB

36891
Dec. '58

University of Chicago Press · Chicago 37
Agent: Cambridge University Press · London

PREFACE

THIS STUDY IS VERY MUCH A BY-PRODUCT OF MY research for *The Jacobean and Caroline Stage*. While reading seventeenth-century documents, I kept track of all mentions of Jacobean and Caroline plays and playwrights in order that I might have solid evidence for later remarks on the reputations of the various dramatists. At first I assumed that I would not have to bother about Shakespeare and Jonson because practically all references to them had been collected in the two allusion books. After noting a number of omissions, however, I began to check each passage I came across against the collections and to transcribe those not found there.

As my file of transcriptions grew, I came to realize that the two allusion books gave a misleading picture of the respective reputations of their subjects. Of course, I knew in a general way, without adding up the evidence, that Jonson's reputation before the closing of the theaters was greater than Shakespeare's, and I assumed that the chronological distribution of the passages in *The Jonson Allusion-Book* gave a fairly accurate picture of the situation, with about five-eighths of the allusions falling in the forty-six years 1597–1642 and three-eighths in the fifty-eight years 1643–1700. Apparently Jonson's reputation declined rapidly in the last three-fifths of the century while Shakespeare's, on the contrary, rose.

At this stage I dropped the whole project for a month or so, and, for a quite unrelated reason, checked all the early editions of seventeenth-century plays in the University of Chicago Libraries. In going through the front matter of a large number of Restoration plays I noted, somewhat to my surprise, that Jonson was mentioned at least as often as Shakespeare and that a goodly number of the allusions were unrecorded. It appeared that my assumption about the falling-off of Jonson's reputation was all wrong. Then there was nothing for it but to have a look at the publications of the second half of the century. Half-reluctantly and half-eagerly, I went through as many likely volumes from 1650 to 1700 as I could get my hands on and found new Jonson allusions by the hundreds.

In the meantime, as I checked passages in *The Shakspere Allusion-Book*, I could not fail to note how very many of the extracts printed there were not really allusions at all and how far out of their true chronological position many of them were placed. By this time I had enough evidence to suggest, though not to establish, several conclusions: (*a*) The relative number of allusions by seventeenth-century writers to Shakespeare and to Jonson was not what the two allusion books indicated. (*b*) The apparent decline in Jonson's reputation after his death as suggested by the chronological distribution of the passages in *The Jonson-Allusion Book* was illusory. (*c*) There were far fewer valid allusions to Shakespeare and his works in the seventeenth century than *The Shakspere Allusion-Book* suggested.

These conclusions were simply general impressions; as yet I had not gone far enough to be able to make any precise statements. I needed to know just how many allusions, judged by the same standard of validity, had been reported for each man. I needed to know how these allusions were distributed chronologically when all were dated by the same standards. And I needed to know what different kinds of allusions there were and the comparative number of each type. Obviously a passage which simply named Shakespeare, without distinction, in a list of a dozen other authors was much less signifi cant than a poem to his memory which said that his writings could not be praised too much.

Having got this far more or less by accident, I found myself driven to continue the investigation and to collect and sift the material which might resolve the problems raised by my harmless curiosity. This book is the result.

In the course of this somewhat tortuous process of tracing down allusions, of transcribing, classifying, counting, checking, and rechecking, I have encountered the friendly interest and assistance of a number of institutions and individuals—an interest I am flattered to acknowledge. The resources of the Henry E. Huntington Library, the Newberry Library, the University of Chicago Library, the Widener and Houghton libraries of Harvard, and the kindness of their custodians have greatly facilitated my search for and checking of allusions. The Research Committee of the Modern Language Association made a grant toward the expenses of typing and mounting the thousands of passages I have had to use. Research in the humanities is heavily indebted to such institutions—often more than to the universities themselves.

Miss Bertha Hensman and Mr. James Merrin have helped with mounting, checking, and collating and have given of their time far beyond the requirement of the bond. Miss Hensman also brought four new allusions to my attention, voluntarily submitting herself to the curse of "allusion consciousness." Professor Hallett Smith criticized the manuscript, greatly to my profit. (Reviewers of the book might well begin that cherished last paragraph, "In spite of the efforts of Professor Smith, Bentley's native awkwardness and inaccuracy still appear on pages . . . . .") Professor Arthur Friedman read the galleys for Volume I in an attempt to bring the accuracy of those pages up to the high standard of *Modern Philology*.

Constant assistance at all stages of the project, from my first ludicrously inadequate conception of the task to the last line of the Index, has come from my collaborator-assistant. Research has never been a lonely job for me.

G. E. B.

December 12, 1944

TABLE OF CONTENTS

CHAPTER I

THE PROBLEM OF UNDERSTANDING
LITERARY REPUTATIONS

THIS BOOK IS AN ATTEMPT TO UNDERSTAND THE RE-
gard in which Shakespeare and Ben Jonson were held
by their contemporaries and successors in the seventeenth century. Such an understanding, in the complete
sense in which we desire it, is, of course, unattainable,
for the vast majority of Englishmen who witnessed or
read the plays of the two masters left no record of their
pleasure or pain. Many records have no doubt been destroyed, and presumably many others are still unprinted
or unnoted. Yet there remains a sizable body of recorded opinion which has already been collected or which
is here set forth for the first time. With this recorded
opinion I propose to deal.

At the very outset it is well to remember the obvious
fact that writers who seem literary giants to us were
often pigmies in the eyes of their contemporaries, that
phrases which ring unforgettably in our ears tinkled
very small in the ears for which they were written.
Nineteenth-century critics and historians were often
hero-worshipers, and they not infrequently attributed
to a sixteenth- or seventeenth-century masterpiece a
contemporary fame and influence which it certainly
never had in its own age.

This tendency to foist our own critical standards and
literary judgments upon the public of Marlowe or

Milton or Shakespeare is no doubt perfectly natural, but it is nonetheless a gross and dangerous distortion. A devoted and enthusiastic admirer of a great artist of the past can easily mislead generations of students. Such has been the fate, in at least one aspect of his work, of the great Milton scholar, David Masson. Masson, like most readers of Milton, was deeply impressed by *Areopagitica* and sought in the pamphlet literature of the time evidence of the influence of this noble document. His findings may be fairly summarized by some of his own statements.

The effect of Milton's *Areopagitica*, immediately after its publication in November 1644, and throughout the year 1645, seems to have been very considerable. Parliament, indeed, took no formal notice of the eloquent pleading for a repeal of their Licensing Ordinance of June 1643. . . . . But public opinion was affected, and the general agitation for Toleration took more and more the precise and practical form into which Milton's treatise had directed it. . . . . There can be no doubt, however, that as Milton, in his *Areopagitica*, had tried to make the official licensers of books, and especially those of them who were ministers, ashamed of their office, so his reasons and sarcasms, conjoined with the irksomeness of the office itself, did produce an immediate effect among those gentlemen, and modify their official conduct.[1]

For example, one finds that John Lilburne had been a reader of the *Areopagitica*, and had imbibed its lesson, and even its phraseology. . . . . There is proof, in the writings of other Independents and Sectaries, that Milton's jocular specimens of the *imprimaturs* in old books had taken hold of the popular fancy. . . . . On the whole, then, Milton's position among his countrymen from the beginning of 1645 onwards may be defined most accurately by conceiving him to have been, in the special field of letters, or pamphleteering, very much what Cromwell was in the broader and harder field of Army action, and what the younger Vane was, in Cromwell's absence, in the House of Commons.[2]

Now this statement of the great Milton scholar accords well with what a modern reader of Milton's

[1] David Masson, *The Life of John Milton* (1873), III, 431–32.

[2] *Ibid.*, pp. 433–34.

sonorous periods would naturally think their influence must have been. Furthermore, Masson cites evidence of a sort from contemporary documents for his conclusions. Yet a fuller examination of the extant pamphlets of these years has shown how wrong Masson was. William Haller, after extensive reading in the thousands of tracts of the Puritan Revolution preserved in the Thomason Collection at the British Museum and in the McAlpin Collection at Union Theological Seminary, makes a very different and much better-grounded statement about the reception and influence of Milton's work.

It appears incredible that Milton's great plea for freedom of the press should have failed of any mention whatever in the thousands of pages printed at the time and abounding in specific references to hundreds of other publications, but the present writer is constrained to report that after a protracted search he has failed to find a single one. . . . . In the light of these facts, we must dismiss the notion that *Areopagitica* had any appreciable effect on the situation in 1644. Masson surmises that Lilburne had imbibed Milton's lesson and very phraseology, but we have seen Lilburne defending free speech on the pillory as early as 1637, and he might have learned what else he needed to know about liberty from many other publications prior to *Areopagitica*. Masson also thinks that the mock order from the Westminster Assembly, prefixed to *The Arraignment of Mr. Persecution*, was suggested by specimen imprimaturs jocularly cited by Milton. But Overton was modeling his mockery on the Marprelate tracts. Masson's most serious misapprehension is, however, of the effect of *Areopagitica* upon enforcement of the printing ordinance. He would have us believe that by Milton's persuasion the licensers grew more lax. The fact is that from the Adoption of the printing ordinance in 1643, directed against royalists and prelatists, the licensers differed among themselves in their attitude toward the issues that arose between the Presbyterians and their various opponents. As the controversy developed, some naturally leaned further to one side and some to the other, and the pamphleteers meanwhile grew bolder and more numerous. The whole system of censorship in fact tended to break down.[3]

The evidence of contemporary pamphlets points, therefore, to the fol-

---

[3] William Haller (ed.), *Tracts on Liberty in the Puritan Revolution, 1638–1647* (1934), I, 135–36.

lowing conclusions concerning Milton's reputation and influence in the years immediately following 1643. (1) Little or nothing was known of him to the pamphleteers and the general public, save as the author of a scandalous book [*The Doctrine and Discipline of Divorce*] which was widely condemned but not widely read. (2) Since none of the critics of the divorce tract seems to have had any personal knowledge of Milton, even of his marital difficulties, we are led to infer that he refrained from association with any recognized groups of Independents, sectaries or Levellers. (3) *Areopagitica* . . . . seems to have attracted no contemporary attention, and to have had no discernible effect.[4]

If Milton idolatry can so distort the place of the man in his time, what can be expected of Shakespeare idolatry? For one hundred and fifty years it has flourished like the bay tree in the land.[5] Many reasons might be cited for thinking that Shakespeare would have had a wider appeal in the seventeenth century than Milton, and certainly some of them are valid; but the surest way to attain any understanding of his contemporary reputation, as of Milton's or Jonson's, is to examine the surviving records of the time.

These records will not, of course, give us Shakespeare's —or any other man's—reputation just as it stood in the years 1601–1700, for we know that many records have been destroyed or lost and that even more comments were never written down. To understand fully the standing of any dramatist in the seventeenth century we should need, for every year in the century, complete records of attendance at public performances of his plays in London and in the provinces, the number of command performances at court, the number of private performances, the number of copies of his works sold and

4 *Ibid.*, p. 139.

5 See, e.g., R.W. Babcock, *The Genesis of Shakespeare Idolatry, 1766–1799* (1931); Charles Knight, *A History of Opinion on the Writings of Shakespeare* (1866); D. Nichol Smith, *Shakespeare in the Eighteenth Century* (1929); Augustus Ralli, *A History of Shakespearian Criticism* (1933).

the number of readers for each copy, all printed statements about the man or his works, all written comments in private papers like letters and commonplace books and diaries, and, finally, records of all unwritten conversations about him. Even such fantastically complete records as these would need others to complement them —weather records and public health records to discount performance figures; printing and literacy records to discount reading and private-papers figures; and a vast amount of biographical and personality records to discount private conversation. Such an impossible mass of evidence would require corresponding figures on other contemporary dramatists for interpretation. Every scholar who writes of the reputation of any figure in the past must be conscious of how far his evidence falls short of such ideal completeness.

Yet some Shakespearean records of all these types do exist—a number surprisingly large considering the remoteness of the time and the status of the drama in the minds of most literate men in the seventeenth century. Similar records exist for Ben Jonson, the contemporary dramatist nearest Shakespeare in stature. A comparison of the numbers and types of these records, decade by decade, ought to give us a clearer picture of Shakespeare's reputation in the seventeenth century than we can now reach by any other means, and the same comparison would display Jonson's standing as well.

A good part of the extant records in these various classes mentioned above have been collected at one time and another into allusion books.[6] A certain num-

---

[6] The various collections of allusions to Shakespeare and Jonson are discussed in chap. iii.

ber of new allusions to Shakspeare and Jonson and their works are here set forth for the first time.[7] If we test all these allusions by a single standard of validity and distribute them into decades and types, we have a body of material, reliable though incomplete, upon which we can base a sounder estimate of the reputations of Shakespeare and Jonson than any other which has been offered. Such testing, distribution, and analysis of the results is the purpose of the succeeding chapters.

[7] See Vol. II, Parts I and II.

CHAPTER II

WHAT IS AN ALLUSION?

THE FIRST PROBLEM TO CONFRONT THE ALLUSION-chaser is the necessity for a definition sufficiently exact to enable him to identify his quarry. Unfortunately, collectors of allusions have not always faced this problem. *The Shakspere Allusion-Book* reprints as allusions scores of passages from the works of sixteenth- and seventeenth-century writers which have seemed to some readers to echo Shakespeare's words, his ideas, or situations in his plays. To take these passages as allusions to Shakespeare is in many cases a highly dubious procedure and in some patently absurd.[1] There are,

---

[1] It is suggested, for instance, that when Webster had his Cornelia say

"Will you make mee such a foole? heere's a white hand:
Can bloud so soone bee washt out?" (*The White Devil*, V, 4, 76–77)

he was imitating Shakespeare's

"Will all great Neptune's ocean wash this blood
Clean from my hand? No. This my hand will rather
The multitudinous seas incarnadine,
Making the green one red" (*Macbeth*, II, 2, 60–64);

and that Middleton's

"MISTRESS PURGE: Husband, I see you are hoodwinked in the right use of feeling and knowledge,—as if I knew you not then as well as the child knows his own father!" (*The Family of Love*, V, 3)

is an imitation of Falstaff's

"By the Lord, I knew ye as well as he that made ye"
(*Henry IV, Part I*, II, 4, 295–96).

There are equally dubious examples from Dekker (*The Shakspere Allusion-Book*, I, 106), from Marston (I, 108, 131, 153), from Webster (I, 115–19), from Middleton (I, 110, 141–44), from Heywood (I, 146, 165, 232; II, 40), from Beaumont and Fletcher (I, 196–203, 283), from Massinger (I, 296–304, 359), from Chapman (I, 170), from Jonson (I, 333), and from Shirley (I, 357).

for instance, many stock situations and characters in the Elizabethan drama which were used over and over again by most of the dramatists of the time, including William Shakespeare.[2] There is no reason to think that Fletcher or Massinger imitated Shakespeare whenever he used one of these stock situations, or even that he imitated Edwards or Kyd or Greene or Lyly, who used them before Shakespeare did. One might even hazard the generalization that Elizabethan playwrights, like modern ones, were much less self-conscious in their use of sources than scholars are likely to think.

Many passages in *The Shakspere Allusion-Book* alleged to be deliberate echoes of Shakespeare's words or sentiments are just as dubious as some said to reflect his situations and characters. Shakespeare, like other Elizabethan dramatists, made constant use of proverbial expressions. When a later dramatist employs one of the same proverbial expressions or comparisons which Shakespeare has put into the mouth of a character, there is no evidence of imitation of Shakespeare, and therefore no allusion.[3]

[2] See the tracing of a number of these situations and characters through many plays in Robert Stanley Forsythe's *The Relations of Shirley's Plays to the Elizabethan Drama* (1914).

[3] Massinger need never have seen or read *As You Like It* to have written
                        "Are you on the stage,
You talk so boldly?
    PARIS: The whole world being one
This place is not exempted"
        (*The Roman Actor*, I, 3; see *The Shakspere Allusion-Book*, I, 302).
Edwards had made the same comparison in *Damon and Pythias* (II, 3) some thirty years before Shakespeare did, and Edwards attributed the comparison to Pythagoras.

In the same way Massinger's passage of the gods smiling at lovers' perjuries (*The Parliament of Love*, V, 1; *The Shakspere Allusion-Book*, I, 301) probably did not come from *Romeo and Juliet*; for Robert Greene had used it, as well as various

This difficulty of allusions which do not allude is, of course, particularly acute in the case of Shakespeare. The situations, characters, and lines of his plays have long been more familiar than any others in English literature except, perhaps, those of the King James translation of the Bible. Consequently, similarities to his work are more frequently noted and commented upon than similarities to any others. All too often readers of Shakespeare are not content simply to point out the resemblances but must insist that they have found clear-cut allusions to Shakespeare or imitations of his lines. A number of these dubious allusions have, unfortunately, found their way into *The Shakspere Allusion-Book*.

As for Jonson, far fewer readers have found themselves sufficiently conversant with his lines to note similarities in the works of other writers.[4] Moreover, there has been no modern idolatry and no jealous pressing of admirers' claims that he was all things to all men in all times. Consequently, the parallel passages printed in *The Jonson Allusion-Book* are very few. This is not to say that only genuine Jonson allusions appear in that collection. Jonson's familiar pugnacity and the known number of his enemies have made scholars overeager to identify him with any unnamed object of satirical

---

classic writers. Even *The Shakspere Allusion-Book* itself notes at another point (I, 189 n.) that the proverb is found in Ovid. For other examples see Morris Palmer Tilly, *Elizabethan Proverb Lore in Lyly's Euphues and in Pettie's Petite Pallace with Parallels from Shakespeare* (1926); see also *The Shakspere Allusion-Book*, II, 39, 70.

[4] The most familiar extended list of Jonsonian parallels is that found in William Dinsmore Briggs's "The Influence of Jonson's Tragedy in the Seventeenth Century," *Anglia*, XXXV (1912), 277-337. The great majority of these parallels are not sufficiently close or distinctive to be called allusions. Only 4 of the 174 have been counted in my totals of Jonson allusions.

attack. Occasionally, as in the case of Dekker's *Satiro-mastix*, there is abundant external evidence to prove that Jonson was indeed the object of the attack; but more often the unspecified victim might equally well, or better, have been someone else.[5]

After much puzzling over passages which have been printed as Shakespeare or Jonson allusions but which actually present no evidence that the authors had either of the great dramatists in mind, I have settled on a series of tests for allusions. On the one hand, an acceptable allusion must mention the name of Jonson or Shakespeare or the name of one of their compositions or characters, or it must contain at least one line quoted from their works.[6] About 98 per cent of the 3,269 Shake-

<hr/>

[5] A good instance in point is Thomas Heywood's sneer in the "Epistle to the Reader" of the 1633 quarto of *The English Traveller: "True it is, that my Playes are not exposed vnto the world in Volumes, to beare the title of* Workes, *(as others)" (The Jonson Allusion-Book*, p. 175). Now the ridicule of Jonson for calling the 1616 edition of his plays, epigrams, poems, entertainments, and masques *The Workes of Beniamin Jonson* is endless (see *The Jonson Allusion-Book*, pp. 119, 196, 271, 319, 486–87, and Vol. II, pp. 35, 108, 111). In any year before 1633 such ridicule necessarily applies to Jonson, for before that year no collection of English plays except his had been called *"Works."* But in the year of Heywood's complaint two other collections of plays which used the pretentious title had appeared: *Certaine Learned and Elegant Workes of the Right Honorable Fulke Lord Brooke* (1633) and *The Workes of Mr. Iohn Marston* (1633). Since the Greville volume had been licensed in the Stationers' Register eight months before *The English Traveller*, Heywood very probably had seen it, and he may well have known of the Marston collection, too. His sneer, therefore, is not certainly aimed at Jonson; indeed, considering the recency of the other publications, it is rather more likely to refer to them. For other doubtful satiric references see *The Jonson Allusion-Book*, pp. 9–10, 11, 29–32, 33, 54.

[6] To be really meticulous, of course, one must refrain from calling any passage a quotation from Shakespeare or Jonson unless the writer specifically acknowledges that he is quoting from one of them (I am speaking here of passages too brief to be absolutely and infallibly identified as coming from either of the two great dramatists), for in spite of a teasingly close similarity to Shakespeare's or Jonson's lines the passage may be completely original or even an echo or lifting from the work of another author. The strict application of this principle, however, would be sheer pedantry; and, though I have longed for strict rules and uncontrovertible principles in setting up the tests for validity, I have been sufficiently indiscriminate to accept as a quotation any passage of one full line or more which first appeared, so far as we know, in a work of Shakespeare or Jonson, whether credited to him or not.

speare and Jonson allusions which I have accepted and classified conform to these requirements. In the other 2 per cent, exceptions have been allowed because external evidence makes it clear that one of the dramatists or his work is referred to, even though no names are mentioned. Most of these exceptions are descriptions of Horace in *Satiromastix* or descriptions of preparations for or performances of masques not named but known from external evidence to have been Jonson's.

On the other hand, certain types of passages which specifically mention the playwrights have been systematically excluded. Title-pages of a man's own works, Stationers' Register entries of those works, publishers' advertisements, and sale catalogues have all been eliminated. These are publishing records and not allusions; and, though they are assuredly evidence of popularity, they belong in bibliographical studies— where they have all been competently treated—and not in allusion books. Publication records of apocryphal plays, on the other hand, are allusions, because a false attribution on a title-page is an attempt to sell a book, usually fraudulently, by an appeal to the public which recognizes the author. Such an appeal goes beyond a mere publishing record; like a quotation it is an attempt to exploit the reputation of Shakespeare or Jonson. It is therefore in the nature of an allusion and has been counted as such.[7]

There are, of course, a number of cases in which special precautions have to be observed in the application of these standards. Restoration revisions of Shake-

[7] By the same token, the mention of Shakespeare or Jonson on title-pages but not as author constitutes an allusion, e.g, the title-pages of *Jonsonus Virbius* (1638) or of *The Poems of Ben Jonson Junior* (1672).

speare's plays and drolls have been treated as if they were canonical works; that is, publication records have not been counted as allusions, but other references to these works have been counted as allusions to the plays from which they are derived.[8] Again, there are a number of passages which mention mythological or historical characters appearing in Shakespeare's or Jonson's plays but by no means in these plays alone. Such figures as Venus, Adonis, Caesar, Brutus, Antony, Cleopatra, Troilus, Cressida, Portia, Sejanus, Catiline, Richard III, Henry VIII, etc., may be referred to as historical or legendary personages without any trace of an allusion to a play. Usually it is perfectly clear that no reference to creations of Shakespeare or Jonson is involved, and no one has claimed the passage as an allusion; but several such references have been included in *The Shakspere Allusion-Book* which probably do not refer to Shakespeare.[9] On this point I have followed the principle that when there is reasonable doubt about the passage it must be eliminated.

Finally, I have restricted allusions to those found in English books and manuscripts.

In the matter of chronological limits, I have maintained narrower restrictions than some of the allusion collections have set up. All allusions considered in this study must have been published (if in printed books) or written (if extant only in manuscript) between the years 1601 and 1700 inclusive. The year 1700 as a terminal date has been generally used and needs no defense.

[8] In many cases it is not possible to tell whether an allusion refers to a Restoration revision of a Shakespearean play or to the folio text (see below, pp. 108–11).

[9] See, e.g., the passages mentioning Lucrece (I, 96; II, 295), Cressida (I, 128), Venus and Adonis (I, 178, 256), Cleopatra (I, 262), and Timon (II, 416).

The elimination of sixteenth-century allusions perhaps requires some explanation as being less familiar. The first and least defensible reason is the concentration of my own interest in the seventeenth century. The second and more considerable is the fact that this study is intended primarily as a comparison of two great literary reputations. Since Shakespeare was born ten years before Jonson and began writing several years before him, it is very difficult to assess the significance of the difference in the Shakespeare and Jonson allusions in the sixteenth century. How much is due to the fact that Jonson probably had not written anything except school exercises by the date of the first Shakespeare allusion? How much is due to the fact that when Francis Meres published *Palladis Tamia* he might have seen nearly half the plays of the currently accepted Shakespeare canon, but very little of Jonson, since 95 per cent of the Jonson canon was still unwritten? Furthermore, in Renaissance society courtly groups were the most articulate. In comparing early allusions, then, how can one allow for the fact that most of Shakespeare's work appealing to the courtly group was written in the sixteenth century, nearly all of Jonson's in the seventeenth?

These and similar difficulties of comparison are for the most part avoided by eliminating sixteenth-century allusions from consideration. Even at the beginning of the seventeenth century, certain of the difficulties still exist, for reputations are cumulative. In the last year of Elizabeth, Shakespeare's writing career was more than half-finished; none of Jonson's greatest comedies and none of his masques had yet been written. A comparison of the allusions to the two men between 1601 and 1700, then, only minimizes and does not wholly obviate the difficulty posed by the earlier date of Shakespeare's work.

The chronological restrictions placed on allusions sometimes raise a problem of dating. What is the proper date for an allusion—date of composition, date of licensing for the stage in the case of a play, date of licensing for the press, or date of printing? Obviously, the date of composition is the real date of the occurrence of the allusion; but in the great majority of cases, probably nine-tenths, there is no generally accepted date of composition. The date of licensing for the stage or the press, being nearest to the date of composition, would be second choice; but for perhaps half the allusions there is no recorded date of licensing for the press and for four-fifths of them no date of licensing for the stage. A consistent attempt, therefore, to organize a mass of allusions on the basis of composition or licensing dates leads to chaos. Thus in *The Shakspere Allusion-Book*, in which all three methods of dating are used with a fine impartiality,[10] one can never tell how many of a group of allusions dated in the third decade of the century were printed then. If Shakespeare allusions so dated are compared, as in this study, with Jonson allusions of the same decade, the comparison goes very much askew because of the variety in the dating methods employed.

---

[10] As well as a wholly indefensible practice of occasionally abandoning the classification-by-date system entirely and grouping allusions by author, as for example, Webster (I, 115–19), Beaumont and Fletcher (I, 196–203), Burton (I, 281–82), Herbert (I, 321–24), Massinger (I, 296–304), Pepys (II, 89–97), Dryden (II, 174–80), Lee (II, 264); or even by subject (I, 32–40).

Faced with this difficulty, I have revised the dating of the entire body of Shakespeare and Jonson allusions used and have classified each allusion by the date of its first printing, with two exceptions. First, in the case of manuscript allusions, where no printing date, of course, is available, I have had to fall back upon the date assigned to the manuscript by its editor or cata loguer. Second, in the very few instances in which an author has himself given the precise date of composition—mostly dated letters—that date has been accepted.

These principles of dating and classification have occasionally led to the inclusion of passages not given seventeenth-century dates in the allusion collections and to the exclusion of others which have been so dated. For instance, Richard Carew's praise of English writers, including Shakespeare, in his *Excellencie of the English Tongue*, which is dated 1595-96 in *The Shakspere Allusion-Book*, is considered here as a seventeenth-century allusion, for it was first published when Camden included it in the second edition of his *Remaines concerning Britaine* in 1614. On the other hand, the account of the conversation between Ben Jonson, Mr. Hales of Eton, and others, which *The Jonson Allusion-Book* prints under the date "about 1633," is excluded entirely; for, though it concerns an event of the early seventeenth century, it was first printed by Nicholas Rowe in the life of Shakespeare published in his edition of 1709.

I hope that this all does not sound like wilful juggling. For a study of this sort it was necessary to have exact and rigid rules by which to consider the thousands of passages, and I have arrived at the above system only after considering and trying a great many others; I believe the criteria here set forth to be the strictest and most defensible of all those I examined. They are not whimsical, but utilitarian, though occasionally their exact application, as in the Rowe quotation just instanced, leads to decisions which are, at first blush, puzzling. I have tried to wander through the maze of allusions with the jewel of consistency to guide me; I hope the reader can follow with confidence and comprehension.

CHAPTER III

THE COLLECTIONS OF SHAKESPEARE AND JONSON ALLUSIONS

IN THE SEVENTY YEARS SINCE C. M. INGLEBY PUBLISHED his *Shakspere Allusion-Books*, Part I, a number of collections of allusions to Shakespeare and Jonson have appeared. Anyone reviewing these collections is most forcibly struck by the number and particularly by the diversity of readers—historians, librarians, public officials, English scholars, publishers, clergymen, lawyers, booksellers, general readers—who have reported Shakespeare allusions, as compared with the handful of professional scholars who have been concerned with references to Jonson. One hundred and twenty-seven individuals have contributed Shakespeare allusions to the ten principal collections used for this study, while all the Jonson allusions are the results of the observations of nine scholars, and all but about 200 of the 2,225 Jonson allusions examined for this book have been reported by only three searchers.[1]

[1] The various collections of Shakespeare allusions acknowledge contributions by the following readers: C. R. Baskervill, E. F. Bates, Thomas Bayne, Edward Bensly, G. E. Bentley, "Bibliothecary," G. Binz, Thomas Birch, A. C. Bradley, John Brant, Rudolph Brotanek, H. Brown, Rawdon Brown, C. Elliot Browne, John Bruce, A. H. Bullen, George Bullen, D. B. Brightwell, C. B. Carew, George Chalmers, Sir Edmund Chambers, W. Chappell, William Chetwood, Andrew Clark, Charles Crawford, Peter Cunningham, J. P. Collier, G. L. Craik, P. A. Daniel, R. K. Dent, Bertrand Dobell, Edward Dowden, Alexander Dyce, J. W. Ebsworth, C. Edmonds, Karl Elze, Arundell Esdaile, Herbert Evans, C. H. Firth, F. G. Fleay, E. Fox, P. S. Furness, F. J. Furnivall, R. Garnett, Mr. Gilson, Sir Israel Gollancz, A. B. Grosart, C. Haines, J. W. Hales, J. O. Halliwell-Phillipps, H. C. Hart, C. S. Harris, Edward B. Harris, W. C. Hazlitt, Bertha Hensman, Charles S. Herpich, J. N. Hetherington,

One sure conclusion is to be drawn from a comparison of the size and variety of these two groups, namely, that a much higher proportion of all the existing allusions to Shakespeare written before 1701 has now been found, collected, and published than of the Jonson allusions. Considering the tremendous interest in Shakespeare in the nineteenth and twentieth centuries, one sees at once that this was inevitable. Whatever the primary interests of a student reading the printed books or manuscript remains of the sixteenth and seventeenth centuries, he is sure to have read or at least heard of Shakespeare and to be brought up short by a mention of his name. And the less literary the character of the text, the more likely the reader is to stop and comment upon the allusion and report it—generally, it would appear from the annotations in the allusions books, to some member of the New Shakspere Society. And not only is Shakespeare's name arresting, but his works have

---

E. H. Hickey, H. A. Holden, Joseph Hunter, Alfred H. Huth, C. M. Ingleby, William Jaggard, Maurice Jones, J. J. Jusserand, W. P. Ker, Joseph Knight, Emil Koppel, Maria Latrielle, Sir Sidney Lee, H. Littledale, P. A. Lyons, W. D. Macray, Margaret Macalister, R. B. McKerrow, Edmund Malone, John M. Manly, Mr. Massey, Paul Meyer, John Munro, Brinsley Nicholson, A. C. P., W. G. P., Sir T. Philips, Emma Phipson, Bernard Quaritch, R. R., Isaac Reed, R. Roberts, T. Rodd, Hyder E. Rollins, A. S. W. Rosenbach, F. J. Routledge, Nicholas Rowe, T. Rundall, Walter Rye, H. E. S., R. Savage, Edward J. L. Scott, W. D. Selby, C. Severn, Richard Simpson, Richard Sims, G. C. Moore Smith, Lucy Toulmin Smith, Teena Rochfort Smith, J. Spedding, Caroline Spurgeon, Howard Staunton, George Steevens, Leslie Stephen, W. H. Stevenson, H. P. Stokes, W. G. Stone, Mrs. C. C. Stopes, D. L. Thomas, G. Thorn-Drury, Morris Tilley, Samuel Timmins, W. S. W. Vaux, E. Viles, C. W. Wallace, Joseph Warton, P. Whatley, F. P. Wilson, Aldis Wright, and E. Yardley.

The nine collectors of Jonson allusions are J. Q. Adams, Jesse Franklin Bradley, W. D. Briggs, C. B. Graham, Thornton Shirley Graves, Howard P. Vincent, Bernard Wagner, Miss Bertha Hensman, who has brought two Jonson and two Shakespeare allusions to my attention, and myself. The two passages published by Arthur Melville Clark and Don Cameron Allen (see p. 36, n. 32) have not been accepted as valid allusions, and I have therefore not counted them.

grown so familiar that all his titles, many of his characters, and hundreds of his lines are widely recognized; general readers have consequently been able to identify them in commonplace books, correspondence, sermons, songbooks, histories, diaries, newspapers, and treatises.

Jonson, on the other hand, has had no such public. The unexpected appearance of his name tingles no spine except that of an occasional overly enthusiastic student of the drama; the very commonness of his patronymic helps to obscure him. The titles of many of his works are little known. The literate reader who thinks "Shakespeare!" at once when he sees mention of *The Two Gentlemen of Verona* or *Measure for Measure, Coriolanus* or *All's Well That Ends Well*, is merely puzzled at the sight of *The Case Is Altered* or *A Tale of a Tub, Cynthia's Revels* or *The Magnetic Lady*. The names of Jonsonian characters casually mentioned in seventeenth-century documents are even less familiar to the modern general reader. It might be amusing to make an academic parlor game of the demonstration of this fact. In the allusions so far recorded from the seventeenth century, the following characters—half Jonson's, half Shakespeare's—are each mentioned from two to seven times. In that century they were apparently about equally familiar, though the total number of allusions to the seven Jonson characters adds up to more than the total for the seven Shakespeare characters. The object of the demonstration-game would be to see how many of these characters can be adequately identified by any well-read individual and then to compare the familiarity of the two groups. The characters in ascending order of seventeenth-century popularity are Shylock, King

Lear, Mercutio, Fly, Romeo, Pug, Bottom, Ursula, Asper, Adam Overdo, Juliet, Crispinus, Polonius, Captain Otter.[2]

In the comparative familiarity of the lines of the two writers, the discrepancy is greatest of all. Most readers have committed to memory at least a few lines of Shakespeare; and they can recognize, if they cannot repeat, scores of passages from the plays and the sonnets. Probably the same readers could recognize or even repeat any stanza of "To Celia" and possibly a few other lines from Jonson's most popular poems, but who knows the lines from his plays? Of all forms of seventeenth-century allusion to Jonson, quotations from his works are the most likely to go unnoted unless they are identified in the text.[3] This fact is of great importance in considering the significance of the comparative number of quotations from Jonson and from Shakespeare recorded in the collections of seventeenth-century allusions.[4]

There can be no doubt, then, that many more allusions to Jonson than to Shakespeare remain to be discovered and recorded.[5] All comparisons of the number of allusions to the two dramatists must discount the figures accordingly. In any category which now shows

[2] Complete figures on the number of seventeenth-century allusions to the characters of the two dramatists are given below, pp. 120 ff.

[3] The comparative popular familiarity of the lines of the two dramatists is well illustrated by the selections in the last (1939) edition of Bartlett's *Familiar Quotations*, which devotes 77 pages to 1,849 quotations from Shakespeare, 2 pages to 41 quotations from Jonson.

[4] See below, pp. 73–80.

[5] Especially in the last three decades of the century, where a much smaller proportion of the extant literature has been examined for Jonson allusions than in the earlier decades.

more allusions to Jonson than to Shakespeare, the preponderance is probably actually greater than the present figures indicate; in categories in which there is little present difference in the figures, allusions yet to be found would probably push Jonson into the lead; in categories in which there are now a great many more Shakespeare allusions, the undiscovered references would probably cut down Shakespeare's dominance.

SHAKESPEARE COLLECTIONS

A little less than two-thirds of the seventeenth-century allusions to Shakespeare and to Jonson which form the basis of this study have appeared in various gatherings of my predecessors. The collections of Shakespeare allusions I have used are as follows:

C. M. INGLEBY. *Shakspere Allusion-Books*, Part I. "New Shakspere Society Publications." London, 1874.

———. *Shakespeare's Centurie of Prayse*. 2d ed. "New Shakspere Society Publications." London, 1879.

FREDERICK J. FURNIVALL. *Some 300 Fresh Allusions to Shakspere.* "New Shakspere Society Publications." London, 1886.

JOHN MUNRO. *The Shakspere Allusion-Book* . . . . *Reissued with a Preface by Sir Edmund Chambers.* Oxford, 1932.

———. "More Shakspere Allusions," *Modern Philology*, XIII (January, 1916), 129–76.

[G. THORN-DRURY]. *Some Seventeenth Century Allusions to Shakespeare and His Works Not Hitherto Collected.* London, 1920.

HYDER E. ROLLINS. "Shakespeare Allusions," *Notes and Queries: Twelfth Series*, X (1922), 224–25.

[G. THORN-DRURY]. *More Seventeenth Century Allusions to Shakespeare and His Works Not Hitherto Collected.* London, 1924.

SIR EDMUND CHAMBERS. *William Shakespeare*, Vol. II (Oxford, 1930), Appens. A, B, and C.

These collections contain many passages which I have not used at all because, according to my definition,[6]

---

[6] See above, pp. 10–16.

they are not allusions—that is, they are parallel passages or publication records or common sayings—or they do not properly fall within the limits of the seventeenth century. It is therefore necessary to consider each collection in turn and to indicate the number of allusions accepted and the number rejected, with the reasons for the rejections.

"THE SHAKSPERE ALLUSION-BOOK"

All the valid passages of the first three collections were reprinted in *The Shakspere Allusion-Book* of 1909, and all that volume, in turn, was reprinted without revision in the last edition of 1932. A discussion of *The Shakspere Allusion-Book* of 1932, therefore, covers all the other four; that collection, furthermore, is the standard familiar one.

The principal defects of the collection are the natural results of the method of its compilation. As John Munro pointed out in his Preface to the edition of 1909, "These volumes were not made in a day. Thirty years have passed in their compilation, and the thousands of books from which their contents have been drawn stretch over three hundred years. Many willing hands, too, have lent assistance. Antiquaries, scholars, and friendly readers, have all most kindly helped." Unfortunately, the many willing hands had many different standards of what constituted an allusion, of what constituted a proper reference, and of what system of dating was to be used; and the editors made no very thorough attempt to reduce them all to order. Consequently, the collection is somewhat chaotic, even printing a number of its

passages in more than one place.[7] For the purposes of
this study, each passage in *The Shakspere Allusion-Book*
has been examined according to the standards set up
for a valid seventeenth-century allusion to Shakespeare
or Jonson. The valid allusions have been redated where
necessary, and all have been classified according to
type by decades.

The examination has resulted in the rejection of a
great many of the passages in this standard collection
of Shakespeare allusions. The group most easily eliminated is the one made up of those passages first printed
before 1601 or after 1700, and of those found in manuscripts dated outside the period by their editors. Five
hundred and three of the passages in *The Shakspere
Allusion-Book* have been eliminated by the date test;
some of them are dated within the seventeenth century
in the collection but fall outside that period when redated according to the principles set up here.[8] Most of
the passages in this rather large group of rejections are
one- or two-line quotations from Shakespeare's works
reprinted in early anthologies like *England's Parnassus*
and *Belvedere* and presented in Appendixes B, C, and D
of *The Shakspere Allusion-Book*.

Another large number of passages has been rejected
because they are not allusions but mere parallel passages, usually very far-fetched parallels. They have

[7] See *The Shakspere Allusion-Book*, I, 198 and 328, 291 and 345, 466 and 526; I,
73, and II, 494; I, 72, and II, 478; II, 180 and 393; I, 418 and II, 468; II, 33 and
469; II, 121 and 469.

[8] A large number of these passages are not true allusions anyhow, but if they fall
outside the seventeenth century no attempt has been made to classify them further.

been discarded, as in the case of Jonson, unless there is as much as one line quoted or a mention of the author's name or the name of one of his works or characters. Two hundred and seventy-two passages have been rejected, the great majority of them, 229, from Volume I.[9]

A number of passages have been eliminated because, though they do mention the names of Shakespeare's characters or works, the names are too common to refer certainly to his creations and there is no other indication that the writer of the passage had Shakespeare in mind. This standard is a difficult one to apply. Unfortunately, there are more than a hundred characters, plays, or poems of Shakespeare which bear the names of familiar historical or mythological figures. When a writer mentions Julius Caesar or Richard III or Venus and Adonis, he does not necessarily have Shakespeare in mind. Even when a title is mentioned as that of a play, the allusion is not always clear, especially in the case of *Richard III* and *Hamlet*, where other plays of the name are known. On the whole, I have tended to exclude in case of doubt, though I suspect myself of having been overindulgent in the case of *Hamlet*. Altogether, 44 passages mentioning the names of Shakespearean creations have been discarded because reference to Shakespeare seemed doubtful.

A number of the passages in *The Shakspere Allusion-Book* are what I have called publishing records and not allusions—title-pages of Shakespeare's own works, Stationers' Register entries, publishers' advertisements, and sale catalogues. If such records use the name of the dramatist incidentally or inaccurately, as in the title

---

[9] See above, p. 7, n. 1, and p. 8, n. 3.

The Poems of Ben Jonson Junior (1672), or refer to apocryphal plays, then there is an allusion; but ordinary publishing and advertising records have been eliminated. Two hundred and ninety-three passages in *The Shakspere Allusion-Book* have been eliminated on these grounds.[10]

Twenty-six passages have been eliminated because, though they do use Shakespeare's words, Shakespeare himself was quoting a proverbial saying. Such passages are adequately illustrated in chapter ii.[11]

Another group of passages has gone into the discard because, though they do not fall exactly into any of the foregoing classifications, they are still too vague and uncertain to be accepted as genuine allusions. The title-page of *The True Chronicle Historie of the Whole Life and Death of Thomas Lord Cromwell*, which says that the play was "Written by W. S.," is an example, for "W. S." may refer to a number of men other than William Shakespeare.[12] Similarly, the satiric passages about Studioso in *The Return from Parnassus*[13] are not sufficiently clear to be accepted as certain references to Shakespeare. Twenty-one such passages in *The Shakspere Allusion-Book* have been rejected.

Finally, a small group of passages has been discarded because they were duplicates or foreign, not English,

[10] In this figure are included the title-pages and other publishing records of drolls and Restoration adaptations of Shakespeare's plays. On the other hand, literary passages referring to these drolls and adaptations have been accepted as genuine allusions to Shakespeare.

[11] See also below, p. 28, n. 17.

[12] On the other hand, the title-page of another apocryphal play, *A Yorkshire Tragedy*, does contain an allusion, for it says that the play was *"Written by* W. Shakspeare."

[13] *The Shakspere Allusion-Book*, I, 155.

allusions or because they were Restoration adaptations of Shakespeare's plays. This last category is the only confusing one. As we have noted, these adaptations have been considered as part of the Shakespeare canon; therefore, any reference to the adaptation is a Shakespeare allusion, but the publication records of the recensions are not, and the adaptation itself is not an allusion. In this miscellaneous group are 16 discarded passages, 11 of them duplicates.

A supplement to *The Shakspere Allusion-Book* is provided in the Preface to the reprint of 1932 written by Sir Edmund Chambers. This Preface presents 14 new allusions[14] not found in the body of the book, most of them taken from the author's own *William Shakespeare*. Of these 14 passages in the Preface, 3 have been rejected because they are sixteenth- rather than seventeenth-century allusions. One other is discarded because it had been printed by Munro in his article, "More Shakspere Allusions," and is here counted as from that source. A fifth passage comes from G. Thorn-Drury's *More Seventeenth Century Allusions to Shakespeare and His Works Not Hitherto Collected* and is counted among Thorn-Drury's valid allusions. Altogether, then, only 9 of the 14 passages in the Preface can be added to the collection of valid allusions.

When all these figures on *The Shakspere Allusion-Book* are assembled, we find a grand total of 2,216 passages presented in that volume as allusions to Shakespeare,[15]

---

[14] Chambers numbers the passages I–XII, but his No. IV contains 3 separate allusions.

[15] Several hundred of these passages come from the appendixes, the Preface, and the notes on other passages. Often the passages cited in the notes are clearer allusions to Shakespeare than those in the body of the work.

of which 1,180 have been rejected for the various reasons assigned. The 1,036 remaining passages constitute the bulk of the valid seventeenth-century allusions to Shakespeare which have been used for this study.

GEORGE THORN-DRURY'S COLLECTIONS

After *The Shakspere Allusion-Book*, the largest collection of passages referring to Shakespeare is that gathered over a number of years by George Thorn-Drury and assembled in two pamphlets, *Some Seventeenth Century Allusions to Shakespeare and His Works Not Hitherto Collected* (London, 1920) and *More Seventeenth Century Allusions to Shakespeare and His Works Not Hitherto Collected* (London, 1924). In these two pamphlets, 254 passages presumably referring to Shakespeare but not found in *The Shakspere Allusion-Book* are set forth. The chronological limits indicated in the titles are strictly observed, and therefore only 1 passage[16] has had to be discarded because of the date of the first edition or manuscript in which it occurs. Publishing records are generally eschewed in these collections, and only one passage—a bookseller's advertisement of *Lucrece*—has been rejected because it falls into this class. A rather large number of passages have been thrown out, however, because they are alleged parallel passages, which really show no clear allusions to Shakespeare's work. Notable are the proverbial expressions quoted from seventeenth-century writers and supposed to derive from Shakespeare, when, as a matter of fact,

---

[16] *More Seventeenth Century Allusions*, p. 20. The passage was first printed in 1704 and therefore could not be accepted, even though it does refer to events before Monmouth's death.

others had used them long before the Swan of Avon.[17]
A total of 25 passages has been eliminated from the
total of 254 because they are quotations of proverbial
expressions rather than quotations of Shakespeare's
work or because they are mere parallel passages whose
parallelism may be doubted. Two further passages
refer to Portia and to Venus, but not necessarily to
Shakespeare's characters of these names. Altogether,
29 passages have been rejected from Thorn-Drury's
total of 254, leaving 225 allusions which may be accepted as valid.

JOHN MUNRO'S "MORE SHAKSPERE ALLUSIONS"

After *The Shakspere Allusion-Book* and Thorn-
Drury's gatherings, the most extensive collection of
allusions is that published by John Munro,[18] the editor
of the 1909 *Allusion-Book*, as a supplement to that
volume. The first source of confusion in this collection
is Munro's reprinting of a number of allusions which
had been published by Thorn-Drury in *Notes and
Queries* and which Thorn-Drury later gathered into his
own two pamphlets.[19] A few of Munro's allusions had
already appeared in *The Shakspere Allusion-Book* but
escaped Munro's attention because they had been

[17] Thorn-Drury found three passages using the proverb "Love will creep where
it cannot go" and attributed them all to imitations of Shakespeare's line in *Two
Gentlemen of Verona* (IV, 2, 19–20). Proteus in this speech actually calls attention
to the fact that he is using a common expression by prefacing the proverbial remark
with the words "for you know that." The proverb, of course, is the old one, "Kynde
[in the sense of 'kindness' or 'love'] will creep where it may not go." *The Oxford Dic-
tionary of English Proverbs* ([Oxford, 1935], pp. 250–51) quotes examples in 1350,
1460, 1500, 1546, and 1548, as well as 1614, 1635, and 1641.

[18] "More Shakspere Allusions," *Modern Philology*, XIII (January, 1916), 497–
544.

[19] A perfectly legitimate procedure on Munro's part, for he published in 1916, and
Thorn-Drury did not collect his allusions until 1920 and 1924.

taken from other editions and were differently dated. Altogether, 63 of Munro's 130[20] have been eliminated because they appeared in other collections. Of the 67 remaining, 4 are dated before the year 1601 and have been thrown out for that reason. Twelve others are mere parallel passages, at best using only three or four of Shakespeare's words. Nine more use the names of characters in Shakespeare's plays and poems—Brutus, Antony, Venus, Adonis, Troilus, Hotspur, Cleopatra— but use them in such a way as to make it unlikely or at best uncertain that the authors had Shakespeare's creations in mind. One is simply the old proverb, "Love will creep where it cannot go," again. Thus of Munro's total of 130 passages, 89 have had to be discarded for one reason or another, leaving only 41 which are valid additions to the collections in *The Shakspere Allusion-Book* and Thorn-Drury's pamphlets.

HYDER ROLLINS' "SHAKESPEARE ALLUSIONS"

Rollins' collection contains 18 passages, 15 of which are valid allusions. Of the other 3, 1 had already appeared in *The Shakspere Allusion-Book*, and 1 is a line which does appear in Shakespeare but which Shakespeare himself had quoted from Marlowe.[21] The other rejected passage is another example of the all-the-world's-a-stage figure used by many poets long before Shakespeare as well as after.

SIR EDMUND CHAMBERS' "WILLIAM SHAKESPEARE"

Appendixes A, B, and C of this monumental work contain allusions to Shakespeare of various kinds.

---

[20] Munro numbers the items 1–86; but his numbers refer to sources, not individual allusions; a number of the books furnished several references.

[21] "Who ever lov'd, that lov'd not at first sight" (*Hero and Leander*, l. 176).

Those in Appendix A are records, mostly from parish registers and legal documents, of the activities of Shakespeare, his ancestors, his friends, and his descendants. Though there are not many references of this type in *The Shakspere Allusion-Book*, those mentioning Shakespeare by name are certainly allusions. Since the passages in this appendix are all biographical records, none naming Shakespeare has been rejected because it was a parallel passage, a publishing record, or a proverbial saying. Only those references failing to mention Shakespeare or dated after 1700 or before 1601 (112 of them) have had to be rejected. There remain 50 valid allusions in Appendix A which are not found in any of the other allusion collections.

The passages in Appendixes B and C are limited to personal references and to contributions to the "Shakespeare-Mythos"; and, since they are not offered as a collection of new allusions, it is not surprising that these two appendixes add very few to the grand total of Shakespeare allusions. There are 203 passages in Appendixes B and C,[22] of which 31 are earlier than 1601 and 78 are later than 1700. Of the remainder, 83 had appeared in previous collections.[23] Seven more are vague and uncertain references to Shakespeare—like those in Jonson's *Poetaster*—or are references to common names, like Sir John Oldcastle, which may or may not be intended for Shakespeare's character. There remain only 4 valid new allusions of the seventeenth

[22] The passages are numbered I–LVIII in one appendix and I–LVIII (*sic*) in the other, but a number contain several distinct allusions.

[23] Really, only 78 had appeared in collections dated before 1930, but 5 of Sir Edmund's new allusions were used by him in his Preface for the reprint of *The Shakspere Allusion-Book* in 1932 and have here been counted as part of that collection.

century to be added to the total from these two appendixes, or 54 from all three.

In these various gatherings a total of 2,983 passages
has been presented. Many of them are duplications,
others fall outside the selected period 1601–1700, and
largest of all is the group which cannot be counted as
valid allusions according to the standards set up in
chapter ii. For one or another of these reasons, 1,612
passages have been discarded, leaving 1,371 valid allusions. This very large number of passages in the
familiar collections which has been rejected after testing
by a well-defined standard is significant. Here we have
one of the reasons for the frequent overestimation of
Shakespeare's influence in his own century. The bulk of
the two volumes of *The Shakspere Allusion-Book* is not
what it seems.

JONSON ALLUSIONS

The collections of Jonson allusions are fewer and
smaller than those of Shakespeare, and from them fewer
allusions have had to be discarded. Both facts arc in-
direct reflections of Shakespeare's popularity in the
last one hundred years. Because of the interest in
Shakespeare, more people have collected allusions to
him than to Jonson; because of the avid interest in and
extensive knowledge of Shakespeare, more people
have wanted to see allusions to him where none exist.
No doubt a further reason for the comparatively small
number of unacceptable Jonson allusions printed has
been the warning example of the Shakespeare collections. The first four, and the largest, Shakespeare
gatherings were printed some years before the first
Jonson collection, and no one can examine the earlier

publications without noting the uncertainty of their standards.

The previously printed collections of Jonson allusions here used are as follows:

JESSE FRANKLIN BRADLEY and JOSEPH QUINCY ADAMS. *The Jonson Allusion-Book*. New Haven, 1922.

THORNTON SHIRLEY GRAVES. "Jonson in the Jest Books," in *Manly Anniversary Studies*. Chicago, 1923.

W. D. BRIGGS. "The Influence of Jonson's Tragedy in the Seventeenth Century," *Anglia*, XXXV (1912), 277–337.

BERNARD WAGNER. "A Jonson Allusion and Others," *Philological Quarterly*, VII (1928), 306–8.

C. B. GRAHAM. "Jonson Allusions in Restoration Comedy," *Review of English Studies*, XV (1939), 200–204.

HOWARD P. VINCENT. "Ben Jonson Allusions," *Notes and Queries*, CLXXVII (1939), 26.

The foremost collection is, of course, *The Jonson Allusion-Book*. This volume contains 861[24] statements about Jonson and his works which have all been tested by the same standards applied to the Shakespeare allusions. Under these tests, 55 of them have been discarded because they do not fall within the period 1601–1700.[25] Fifty-three more have been thrown out because they are what I have called publishing records rather than allusions. Twenty-one others are descriptive passages, generally satiric, which someone has thought

[24] There are not 861 separate entries in the volume, but many of the passages, like those in *The Shakspere Allusion-Book*, are really comprised of several different Jonson allusions, though the printing of the extracts sometimes obscures this fact; note, e.g., the three separate allusions in the lines taken from the Preface to *The Womens Conquest*, pp. 363–64; and the two distinct allusions in the Preface to *Momus triumphans*, p. 418. All passages have been compared with the original to determine whether the references to Jonson are all part of one discussion or independent allusions.

[25] Forty passages appeared before 1601; 14 were not first printed until after 1700, though they have been given seventeenth-century dates in the collection. One is eliminated because it is printed twice under two different dates (pp. 258 and 313). Sixty-nine other passages have been redated, but in these cases both Bradley and Adams' date and mine fall within the seventeenth century.

might have been aimed at Jonson but which do not mention his name or the name of any of his creations and which may equally well refer to various other individuals of the time. Two further passages are references to Beaumont and Fletcher's *The Scornful Lady* from Sir Henry Herbert's office-book, which cannot be allowed as Jonson allusions. Only one extract has been eliminated because it is a parallel passage or situation.

This last figure is most illuminating as evidence of an important fact bearing on the usual estimates of the comparative reputations of Shakespeare and Jonson in their own times. Much of the supposed great reputation of Shakespeare in the seventeenth century is a simple matter of the modern familiarity with his lines. When we read one of the various Jacobean or Caroline or Restoration repetitions of an idea or a figure or a situation, Jonson or Lyly or Heywood never comes to mind, though they may all have used it; but if it ever appeared in however modified a form in any of the thirty-seven plays or poems of Shakespeare, someone is sure to note it and to call attention to the allusion, though more often than not there is no allusion at all. It seems to me that a comparison of the number of parallel passages discarded by precisely the same standards from *The Shakspere Allusion-Book* (272) and from *The Jonson Allusion-Book* (1) is a striking illustration of this fact.

After the passages enumerated have been discarded for the reasons assigned, there remain in *The Jonson Allusion-Book* 729 allusions in the period 1601–1700 which are valid according to the standards set up in chapter ii. These 729 passages are the only Jonson allusions used in the following chapters which will not be found printed in Volume II, Part II. Other Jonson allusions which have been previously published are very few and for convenient reference have been reprinted in Volume II.

After *The Jonson Allusion-Book*, the next largest collection of valid allusions from seventeenth-century sources referring to Jonson and his works[26] is that of C. B. Graham. None of the passages in his collection had appeared in *The Jonson Allusion-Book*. The 16 allusions are all drawn from Restoration comedies printed between 1661 and 1695, though Graham has used production instead of printing dates, and all, accordingly, fall within the chronological limits which have been set up. Since all the passages, moreover, mention Jonson's name or the name of one of his accepted works or characters, the entire collection has been used in this study. All the passages are reprinted in Volume II, each with acknowledgments of Professor Graham's prior claim.

Thornton Shirley Graves's interesting article in *The Manly Anniversary Studies*, "Jonson and the Jest Books," treats Ben as the subject of popular stories—an illuminating phase of his reputation and one in which he completely overshadows Shakespeare.[27] Since Professor Graves's purpose was primarily to trace and classify jokes, the bulk of his passages are drawn from eighteenth- and nineteenth-century publications which fall outside our chronological limits. Of the 89 passages about Jonson which he prints or alludes to, only 8 come

---

[26] I am ignoring my own collection of 152 allusions, which appeared in the *Huntington Library Quarterly*, V (October, 1941), 65–113. This collection was just a preliminary sketch for the present volume—though I did not know it at the time—and the allusions have been distributed where they belong in Vol. II.

[27] See below, pp. 94–98.

from seventeenth-century sources and are not found in *The Jonson Allusion-Book*. Since each of the 8 mentions Jonson by name, they are all valid allusions and are reprinted in Volume II.

W. D. Brigg's survey, "The Influence of Jonson's Tragedy in the Seventeenth Century,"[28] is the only one of the six Jonson studies used which is not intended to be a collection of allusions. In the 174 passages cited, Jonson's name is never mentioned, nor is the name of any of his works or characters. The extracts are all parallel passages intended to show indebtedness to Jonson rather than frank allusion to him. Four of the passages are, however, sufficiently exact quotations of Jonson's own lines to fulfil the requirements of a genuine allusion, and they have been reprinted in Volume II, Part II.[29]

The last two articles used have contributed 1 and 2 allusions, respectively. Bernard Wagner included only 1 passage about Jonson in his article, "A Jonson Allusion and Others,"[30] and this one meets all the requirements which have been set up here. Of the 3 ex-

[28] *Anglia*, XXXV (1912), 277–337.

[29] These rather surprising figures—4 valid allusions in 174 passages—are, it must be pointed out, by no means a refutation of Professor Briggs's contention that Jonson greatly influenced the tragedy of the century. There can be no doubt that the influence of *Catiline* and *Sejanus* was much greater than has been commonly recognized. My own figures on the specific allusions to the two plays are enough to demonstrate this fact (see below, pp. 109–12). My purpose and method and Professor Briggs's are simply different. I am presenting evidence that Jonson was so widely known and admired that hundreds of seventeenth-century writers took it for granted that their readers would be impressed or illuminated by unquestionable allusions to the man and his work; Professor Briggs was trying to show that when seventeenth-century dramatists wrote tragedies they were often instructed by particular scenes and speeches in *Catiline* and *Sejanus*. Our investigations are complementary; the results are not contradictory.

[30] *Philological Quarterly*, VII (1928), 306–8.

tracts in Howard P. Vincent's, "Ben Jonson Allusions,"[31] 2 fall in the seventeenth century; both of
them mention Jonson by name.[32]

Altogether, 1,146 passages have been printed in the
various collections.[33] Three hundred and eighty-six
of them have been eliminated for the reasons specified,
and 760 have been accepted as valid allusions according
to the standards set up.[34] These 760 acceptable Jonson
allusions and the 1,371 valid Shakespeare allusions,
together with the new seventeenth-century allusions
to both poets which I have found,[35] comprise the materials upon which the following discussions of Shakespeare and Jonson's seventeenth-century reputations
are based.

[31] *Notes and Queries*, CLXXVII (1939), 26.

[32] Perhaps mention should be made here of two other passages which have been
printed as Jonson allusions: A. M. Clarke's "Jonson Allusion in Jeremy Taylor,"
Notes and Queries, CXLVIII (1925), 459; and Don Cameron Allen's "A Jonson Allusion," *Times Literary Supplement*, April 18, 1936. The passage from Jeremy Taylor
is not really a Jonson allusion, but a Senecan one, as Edward Bensly pointed out
(*Notes and Queries*, CXLIX [1925], 31). The passage in Allen's note, though suggestive, is much too uncertain to be accepted as an allusion to *The Alchemist* according
to the standards used here.

[33] Including Clarke's and Allen's single passages which are not in collections.

[34] This rejection of 33 per cent is not quite comparable to the rejection of 54 per
cent of the Shakespeare allusions, for the second and third largest Jonson collections
do not pretend to be gatherings of allusions before 1700. Briggs's passages were not
intended as allusions; Graves's jokes had no chronological limits. Excluding these
two collections entirely, only 15 per cent of the passages in the other gatherings
have been rejected.

[35] See Vol. II, Parts I and II.

CHAPTER IV

THE DISTRIBUTION OF ALLUSIONS BY DECADES

THE FAMILIAR COLLECTIONS OF SHAKESPEARE AND Jonson allusions analyzed in the last chapter provide us with 1,371 valid seventeenth-century allusions to Shakespeare and 760 valid seventeenth-century allusions to Jonson. To these totals must be added the new allusions to the two dramatists which I have found and which are printed in Volume II, Parts I and II. These collections contain 59 new allusions to Shakespeare and 1,079 to Jonson, all of them tested by the standards which have been applied to the allusions of the earlier collections.

Judged by the mere number of allusions, then, Jonson's reputation was greater in the seventeenth century, taken as a whole, than Shakespeare's, for there are 1,839 recorded allusions to him and 1,430 to Shakespeare, and certainly many Jonson allusions are still unrecorded. The impression conveyed by the bulk of *The Shakspere Allusion-Book* is misleading; equally misleading is the impression conveyed by the greater number of supplementary collections of allusions to Shakespeare which have appeared.

Chiefly responsible for these erroneous impressions are the large number of false allusions in the Shakespeare collections and the large number of Jonson allusions which have hitherto escaped publication. It is well to remember at this point that there are doubtless many allusions to both men which are still unknown. It cannot be pointed out too often, however, that unquestionably far more allusions to Jonson than to Shakespeare remain to be discovered.

If Jonson's reputation, as indicated by collected allusions, seems greater than Shakespeare's in the seventeenth century as a whole, may it not be that the overall figures are misleading? A great preponderance of Jonson allusions in one decade of the century could obscure the fact that in most decades writers referred more often to Shakespeare. It will be further enlightening, therefore, on this and other scores to examine the distribution of allusions by decades.

1601–10

In the first decade of the seventeenth century one would expect to find more allusions to Shakespeare than to Jonson, because Shakespeare had been before the London audience longer. Nearly all his plays had been performed before 1610; furthermore, by that year all his poems and sixteen of his plays had been presented to the reading public, and some of the favorites had gone through several editions—*Venus and Adonis*, ten; *The Rape of Lucrece*, five; *Richard III*, four; *Henry IV, Part I*, four; *Richard II*, three; *Romeo and Juliet*, three. In contrast, much of Jonson's work had not yet been written, and more was unpublished. Only eight of his plays, six of his masques and entertainments, and none of his poems[1] had been seen in print in the first decade of the century. In spite of the greater advancement of Shakespeare's career in this decade, there are 119 al-

---

[1] Except songs in plays and occasional pieces in anthologies like *Love's Martyr*.

lusions to Jonson in the period as compared to 81 to Shakespeare.

The much greater number of allusions to Jonson is most surprising. It is due in large part to the mention of Jonson in connections in which Shakespeare seldom or never figures. Most noteworthy are the references to the performances or preparations for performances of Jonson's masques. Letters of ambassadors and paid correspondents are full of this subject. Not only were masque performances spectacular occasions patronized by the most conspicuous people in London and therefore widely talked about, but almost all the spectators were literate. The high rate of literacy in Jonson's peculiar audience is a constant factor in the establishment of his reputation.

The next most noteworthy group of Jonson allusions in this decade comes from *Satiromastix* and other satiric jibes at Jonson. Here again is a connection in which Shakespeare is seldom found. Throughout his career, Jonson's sturdy, not to say bellicose, personality made enemies and attracted attention. Before the days of newspapers he was always "good copy," and long after his death he was still referred to in terms half of irritation, half of indulgence. Jonson made an impression both through his genius and through his personality; there are very few contemporary records of the impression made by the personality of "gentle Shakespeare."

Finally, nearly a score of the allusions from this decade are concerned with the performance or the publication of *Sejanus* and *Volpone*. There is no clear evidence that any of the plays of Shakespeare ever made such an impression on his contemporaries as did these two.[2] The significance of the number of references to *Sejanus* and *Volpone* in this particular decade becomes the greater when one remembers that *Hamlet*, *Othello*, *Lear*, and *Macbeth* are all products of the same period. Most of the allusions to the two Jonson plays are entire poems praising them in the highest terms,[3] and a number of them are written by poets of renown. Certainly, this group of allusions is most suggestive of Jonson's great distinction in the first decade of the century.

The Shakespeare allusions in the first decade of the century give no such clear dominance in any type of literary allusion. Most notable are the 17 records of Shakespeare's business and professional activities—his career as a player shown in casts and patents; his connection with property transactions, mostly in and around Stratford; and the appearance of his name in wills. Since there are only 1 or 2 records of this type for Jonson,[4] the discrepancy is marked. The difference seems due to two facts: (1) Shakespeare was obviously (for our general knowledge of Jonson confirms the judgment) more interested in the accumulation of property

---

[2] Throughout the century these plays were more frequently referred to than any of Shakespeare's (see below, pp. 109 ff.).

[3] Most of the poems appeared in the 1605 quarto of *Sejanus* and the 1607 quarto of *Volpone*. This fact brings up the important consideration that Jonson published his own plays, while Shakespeare did not—a distinction which cannot be overemphasized; it colors all phases of the study of the two dramatists. Certainly, much of the difference between the reputations of the two poets in their own century, as well as much of the difference in the study of their works since, has been due to this fact.

[4] In the first decade there are 24 allusions to Jonson in Class 17 (see below, pp. 96–98), but most of them are satirical digs or anecdotes or records of Jonson's unfortunate encounters with the law. Only one can, strictly speaking, be called a business or professional record.

than Jonson was, and (2) C. W. Wallace, Halliwell-Phillipps, Leslie Hotson, and others have ransacked millions of records seeking any barest mention of Shakespeare. There has been no search even remotely comparable for references to Jonson; consequently, more examples of Jonson's contact with legal affairs probably remain undiscovered. (No doubt such records are more likely to concern breaches of the peace, libel, and recusancy than property transactions.) One cannot fail to remark that Shakespeare's lead in records of this type has nothing to do with his literary reputation, though it may be taken as some indication of his repute as a solid man of property.

There are a number of references to Shakespeare's plays and characters in this decade, a few more than to Jonson's. The work most frequently mentioned (5 times) is *Venus and Adonis*, probably Shakespeare's best-known composition between 1590 and 1616; the character most popular in this, as in all other decades of the century,[5] is Falstaff.

1611–20

In the second decade of the century one might expect the Jonson allusions to outnumber the Shakespeare ones, for it was in this period that the first Jonson folio appeared.[6] Indeed, Jonson would not have ventured to publish this collection of his own works had not his reputation been very high. Even as it was, there were

[5] See below, pp. 109 ff.

[6] The obscurity of Shakespeare's death in 1616 has been so often remarked upon that no one will be surprised at the lack of allusion to it. One cannot help noting, however, the sharp contrast with the great outpouring of comment after Jonson's death in 1637.

many sneers at a man who would collect his own plays and who presumed to call them "Works."[7] Never before had such a collection appeared in English.

Between 1611 and 1620 there are recorded 88 allusions to Shakespeare and 103 to Jonson. When these references are sorted, surprisingly few of them seem to be related to the publication of the folio. Once more the largest group of Jonson allusions is made up of references of one kind and another to the masques. Another sizable group consists of allusions to Jonson's characters, which in this decade alone seem more popular than Shakespeare's. The only large group of Jonson allusions peculiar to this decade are those referring to his trip to Edinburgh, but even these are greatly outnumbered by allusions to the masques.

The Shakespeare allusions again are dominated by the business references—records of stock in the Blackfriars and the Globe, of ownership of London and Stratford houses and lands, of concern with the Mountjoy dowry. In this decade, again, there are several times as many such business records of Shakespeare as of Jonson and for the same reasons as before. Other types of allusion are less numerous than the 30-odd business and professional records. There are 11 records of payments for performances of Shakespeare's plays; 7 records of the presence of copies of his plays in private libraries; 4 allusions to Falstaff; 9 quotations from his works; and 4 accounts of the burning of the Globe which mention *Henry VIII* as the play being performed at the time. Characteristically, none of the authors of the fire stories

---

[7] The volume was entitled *The Workes of Beniamin Jonson*. For some of the many jibes at Jonson for his presumption see Vol. II, pp. 111, 123, 243.

which name the play being performed—Wotton or Howes or Lorkins or the anonymous writer of the ballad—thought it worth while to mention the fact that the play was written by William Shakespeare.

1621–30

The third decade is the period of the issue of the famous First Folio of 1623. The modern reader would expect that this, of all events connected with Shakespeare's career, must surely have called forth comments in the literary world. It did, of course; there are more passages praising Shakespeare and poems directed to him in this decade than in the two previous ones together. Yet, even so, the discrepancy between the Jonson and Shakespeare allusions is greater than ever before. There are 108 to Jonson and only 43 to Shakespeare.

Nearly one-third of the Shakespeare allusions is made up of poems or long prose passages in his memory, half of this third printed in the Folio itself. Half a dozen are records of performances of his plays, and about an equal number are quotations from his works. The rest are scattered.

In the case of Jonson, there is, because of his diminished output, a falling-off in the records of performances of his masques and plays—only about one-third as many as in the previous decade. But there is a striking increase in the number of transcripts of his works appearing in commonplace books and manuscript anthologies—nearly twice as many as in the two preceding decades together, and more than for Shakespeare in the whole first half of the century. Other common types of allusions to Jonson in the decade are lines or poems in his praise and personal records.

The situation with regard to Shakespeare and Jonson allusions in this third decade of the seventeenth century is for the modern student of literature the most arresting of all. When the book embodying the greatest achievement of any single volume in all literature appeared, the literate public for which it was issued talked mostly about a fellow named Jonson.

1631–40

The period of the 1630's includes the death of Jonson, and here one might reasonably anticipate that allusions to him would be more numerous than to Shakespeare, as they are. The comparative esteem in which their contemporaries held these two great dramatists is most vividly reflected by the fact that in the five years after Shakespeare's death not a single poem commemorative of that great passing appeared, while in the four years after Jonson's death there were more than fifty.

Altogether, there are 189 allusions to Jonson in this decade and 93 to Shakespeare. The Jonson allusions are, of course, dominated by the poems of the 1638 volume to his memory, *Jonsonus Virbius*, to which most of the distinguished poets of the time contributed. But there are numerous testimonials to him outside that volume in lines alluding to his greatness, though not always devoted primarily to it. There are 22 quotations from his work, as well as 17 records of performances of his plays.

The Shakespeare allusions in this decade are more numerous than in any previous one, even though there are only half as many as to Jonson. A number of verses in his praise are printed in the Second Folio of 1632 and in the *Poems* of 1640. Half a dozen of the poems in *Jonsonus Virbius* also mention Shakespeare, most of them with praise. There are 22 quotations from his works and 10 records of performances of his plays, as well as the usual allusions—this time 6—to Falstaff. The increasing frequency of literary allusions to Shakespeare in this period would be quite notable if he were not so completely overshadowed by Jonson.

1641–50

The fifth decade encompasses the terrible period of civil war. In such a time of national travail one might expect literary allusions almost to cease, especially in Puritan London. They do fall off from the preceding decade, but both the Shakespeare and the Jonson allusions are more numerous than in any of the three periods before the fruitful 1630's: 94 to Shakespeare and 125 to Jonson.

The great restriction of the wars on literary publication came in 1643, 1644, and 1645; and the allusions are correspondingly few in these years, but in 1646 they begin to increase. A large number is found in 1646, 1647, and 1648 in the Shirley, Beaumont and Fletcher, Suckling, Herrick, and Baron publications alone. Most productive of allusions, as one might expect, is the great parade of contemporary poets turned out to honor Beaumont and Fletcher in commendatory verses for the Folio of 1647. There are 20 allusions to the two earlier dramatists in these poems, 13 to Jonson and 7 to Shakespeare. It is significant that the 13:7 ratio in this collection of verses by play-conscious writers is very close to the ratio of all allusions in the previous four decades—519:305.

When the entire body of allusions of the fifth decade of the century is classified according to type, we find that the largest group referring to Shakespeare is made up of those mentioning his characters by name. There are 30 of them, half again as many as in any previous decade. The most popular character, as usual, is Falstaff, with 15 references; no other character of Shakespeare's is mentioned more than twice. Thirty-one of the allusions to Shakespeare in the decade quote from his works, and 3 praise him as a great, or the greatest, English dramatist.

The praise of Jonson as a ranking literary figure is even more common—28 passages offering homage to him. Thirty-nine passages quote from his work, and 36 refer to his plays by name, usually for purposes of illustration. This last group is surprisingly large, considering that the theaters were closed for eight of the ten years in the decade. Perhaps men thought more about particular plays when they could no longer see any in the theaters. Certainly, the publishing records make it clear that play-reading flourished in these years.[8]

1651–60

The decade of the Protectorate is the most astonishing of the century from the point of view of allusions. In this period, when the great outpouring of tracts and pamphlets suggests that every literate man in England took his pen in hand with a stern resolve to reform the

---

[8] See Louis B. Wright, "The Reading of Plays during the Puritan Revolution," *Huntington Library Bulletin*, No. 6 (November, 1934), pp. 73–108.

world, one might expect to find mere playwrights like Shakespeare and Jonson impatiently brushed aside. Yet from 1651 to 1660 there are more allusions to them than in any other decade of the century—630, as compared with the 495 of the articulate 1690's. In a time of stress and avid social and political planning, Englishmen remembered the great poets of their fathers. The allusions to Shakespeare (301) more than triple those of any preceding decade, and those to Jonson (329) double the number in any earlier period except that of his death.

The greatest single factor in this increase is the anthology of passages from plays published by John Cotgrave in 1655 under the title *The English Treasury of Wit and Language*,[9] a book containing 154 extracts from Shakespeare's plays and 111 from Jonson's. But even without Cotgrave there are more allusions in this decade than in any previous one. The highly allusive Gayton has 26, mostly to Jonson, in his *Pleasant Notes on Don Quixote;* there are 37, mostly to Shakespeare, in Poole's *England's Parnassus;* 27, mostly to Jonson, in Cotgrave's *Wits Interpreter;* and about 10 apiece in Cokayne's *Small Poems of Divers Sorts* and *Parnassus Biceps*. A remarkable proportion of these allusions is in the form of quotations published, generally without attribution, in the various anthologies.

Aside from the quotations, the allusions fall in fairly normal numbers into about the usual types. There are 41 praising Jonson as a great, or the greatest, play-

[9] For a discussion of this remarkable anthology see my article, "John Cotgrave's *English Treasury of Wit and Language* and the Elizabethan Drama," *Studies in Philology*, XL (April, 1943), 186–203.

wright, and 7 so designating Shakespeare. Particular
plays of the two dramatists are mentioned 66 times—
Shakespeare's 25 and Jonson's 41; Shakespeare's characters are named 43 times and Jonson's 38. Sixteen of
the Shakespeare allusions concern apocryphal plays
printed under his name in this decade, and 9 Jonson
allusions are found in belated descriptions of his
masques in *Finetti Philoxenis*. Other allusions are a scat-
tering of various types, none particularly notable.

1661–70

After the great outburst of the 1650's, the allusions of
the first decade of the Restoration seem meager; yet the
339 references of the time are really more numerous
than those of any preceding decade except the fifties.
Of that number, 196 refer to Jonson and 143 to Shakespeare. The bulk of them are of familiar types. Jonson is
praised as a great, or the greatest, poet 24 times, Shakespeare 9. There are 137 references to particular plays
of Jonson's, 60 to Shakespeare's. Shakespeare's characters, however, are mentioned 60 times to Jonson's
47. The really notable development of the time is found
in the increase in the number of references to performances of plays—112, several such references often oc-
curring in one passage. Inevitably there would be a
greater number of such allusions than under the Protectorate, but it is surprising to find more than in any other
decade of the century, before or after. It is highly im-
probable that there were actually more performances of
Shakespeare's and Jonson's plays at this time than in
the decade 1601–10, say, but there was certainly more
writing about them. No doubt the relief at the removal

of Commonwealth restrictions contributed to the popularity of writings about plays, but the character of the audience was probably even more significant. Most of Pepys's fellow-patrons at the Theatre Royal could write, and many did; neither literacy nor critical dramatic interest was so common at the Globe.

A large part of these references to performances—59 out of 112[10]—come from the diary of that inveterate but uneasy playgoer, the Clerk of the King's Ships.[11] He mentions 37 Shakespearean performances and 22 Jonsonian ones, all but 6 or 8 of which he attended himself. Though he saw more Shakespeare, in the original or a revised form, he had more praise for Jonson. The plays of Shakespeare which he saw in one form or another were *Hamlet, Henry IV, Part 1, Henry VIII, Macbeth, The Merry Wives of Windsor, A Midsummer-Night's Dream, Othello, Romeo and Juliet, The Taming of the Shrew, The Tempest,* and *Twelfth Night;* some of them he saw several times. The Jonson plays were *The Silent Woman, Bartholomew Fair, The Alchemist, Catiline,* and *Volpone.*

For many of Shakespeare's masterpieces Pepys had nothing good to say. Of *Twelfth Night* he opines: "It be but a silly play" (January 6, 1662/63) and "one of the weakest plays that ever I saw on the stage" (January 20, 1668/69). *Romeo and Juliet* "is a play of itself the worst that ever I heard in my life" (March 1, 1661/62).

---

[10] There are 15 or more other Shakespeare and Jonson allusions in Pepys, but they do not refer to performances.

[11] Even without Pepys's records there would be many more references to performances of plays in this decade than in any other, for in the first two decades of the century when there are 47 and 66 records of performances, respectively, a large number of the allusions concern Jonson's masques, not his plays.

A Midsummer-Night's Dream "is the most insipid ridiculous play that ever I saw in my life" (September 29, 1662). *The Merry Wives of Windsor* "did not please me at all, in no part of it" (August 15, 1667). *The Taming of the Shrew* "hath some very good pieces in it, but generally is but a mean play" (April 9, 1667) and is "a silly play and an old one" (November 1, 1667).

No play of Jonson is ever so roundly condemned. The worst he ever says is found in his remarks on *Catiline*, which he had called "a very excellent piece" when he read it on December 18, 1664. But when he saw a performance of the play on December 19, 1668, he said: "A play of much good sense and words to read, but that do appear the worst upon the stage, I mean, the least diverting, that ever I saw any. . . . . But the play is only to be read." It is most illuminating to note his qualification of his condemnation of Jonson in comparison with his categorical dismissal of *Twelfth Night*, *Romeo and Juliet*, *A Midsummer-Night's Dream*, and *The Merry Wives of Windsor*. Obviously, Pepys felt that Jonson was a classic presumably to be admired, but Shakespeare was not much different from any other dramatist.

This same attitude is apparent in his praise of Jonson and Shakespeare where the effect is reversed: the praise of Shakespeare is qualified, but of Jonson it is categorical. Moreover, it is quite clear that in certain instances the features of the Shakespearean play which he singles out for praise are Restoration additions, while the admirable Jonsonian characteristics are all parts of the original plays. His remarks on *The Tempest* are a case in point; he says it is "the most innocent play that ever

I saw; and a curious piece of musique in an echo of half sentences, the echo repeating the former half, while the man goes on to the latter; which is mighty pretty. The play [has] no great wit, but yet good, above ordinary plays" (November 7, 1667); "saw the Tempest again, which is very pleasant, and full of so good variety that I cannot be more pleased almost in a comedy, only the seamen's part a little too tedious" (November 13, 1667); "which, as often as I have seen it, I do like very well" (December 12, 1667); "which we have often seen, but yet I was pleased again, and shall be again to see it, it is so full of variety, and particularly this day I took pleasure to learn the tune of the seaman's dance, which I have much desired to be perfect in, and have made myself so" (February 3, 1667/68).

His comments on *Macbeth* are similarly mixed. It is "a pretty good play, but admirably acted" (November 5, 1664); "most excellently acted, and a most excellent play for variety" (December 28, 1666); "a most excellent play in all respects, but especially in divertisement, though it be a deep tragedy; which is a strange perfection in a tragedy, it being most proper here, and suitable" (January 7, 1666/67); "it is one of the best plays for a stage, and variety of dancing and musique, that ever I saw" (April 19, 1667); "which we still like mightily, though mighty short of the content we used to have when Betterton acted" (November 6, 1667).

Of *Henry VIII* Pepys says: "Saw the so much cried-up play of 'Henry the Eighth'; which, though I went with resolution to like it, is so simple a thing made up of a great many patches, that, besides the shows and processions in it, there is nothing in the world good or well done. Thence mightily dissatisfied" (January 1, 1663/64); "did see 'King Harry the Eighth'; and was mightily pleased, better than I ever expected, with the history and shows of it" (December 30, 1668).

Hamlet appealed to Pepys as an actor's vehicle. He writes of his attendance at five performances of the great tragedy; but four of the passages say nothing whatsoever about the play, though they contain the highest praise for Betterton, and two say that the whole play was "well performed." In one instance his praise of the acting is so stated as almost to imply that Betterton contributed more than Shakespeare: "Saw 'Hamlett' done, giving us fresh reason never to think enough of Betterton" (May 28, 1663). Only in his last record does Pepys ever hint that the play itself may have been good: "Saw 'Hamlet,' which we have not seen this year before, or more; and mightily pleased with it; but, above all, with Betterton, the best part, I believe, that ever man acted" (August 31, 1668).

After reading all this qualified praise of Shakespeare, one cannot but be impressed with Pepys's wholehearted enthusiasm for *Volpone, The Alchemist, Epicoene,* and *Every Man in His Humour,* and his only half-qualified praise for *Bartholomew Fair.*

Of *Volpone* he says: "A most excellent play; the best I think I ever saw, and well acted" (January 14, 1664/65). *The Alchemist* "is a most incomparable play" (June 22, 1661); "it is still a good play, having not been acted for two or three years before" (April 17, 1669).

Of *Epicoene:* "Saw 'The Silent Woman.' The first time that ever I did see it, and it is an excellent play" (January 7, 1660/61); "to the Theatre, where I saw a piece of 'The Silent Woman,' which pleased me" (May 25, 1661); "saw 'The Silent Woman'; but methought not so well done or so good a play as I formerly thought it to be, or else I am now-a-days out of humour" (June 1, 1664); "I never was more taken with a play than I am with this 'Silent Woman,' as old as it is, and as often as I have seen it. There is more wit in it than goes to ten new plays" (April 16, 1667); "saw 'The Silent Woman'; the best comedy, I think, that was ever wrote; and sitting by Shadwell the poet, he was big with admiration of it" (September 19, 1668).

After reading *Every Man in His Humour*, he says that the play has "the greatest propriety of speech that ever I read in my life" (February 9, 1666/67).

Finally, Pepys's comments on *Bartholomew Fair* show a little of the qualifications with which he tempered his praise of Shakespeare; but the praise is more resounding, and the qualifications seem traceable to the relics of his youthful Puritanism. He says: "Saw 'Bartholomew Faire,' the first time it was acted now-a-days. It is a most admirable play and well acted, but too much prophane and abusive" (June 8, 1661); "and here was 'Bartholomew Fayre,' with the puppet-show, acted to-day, which had not been these forty years . . . . but I do never a whit like it the better for the puppets, but rather the worse" (September 7, 1661); "saw 'Bartholomew Fayre,' which do still please me; and is, as it is acted, the best comedy in the world, I believe" (August 2, 1664); "it is an excellent play; the more I see it, the more I love the wit of it; only the business of abusing the Puritans begins to grow stale, and of no use, they being the people that, at last, will be found the wisest" (September 4, 1668).[12]

Pepys is always winning in his lavish use of superlatives. It is noteworthy that in these passages most of the superlatives are used to express the unexampled badness of Shakespeare's plays and the unexampled excellence of Jonson's. The little man from the Admiralty was not an unusually perceptive or judicious critic, but his comments ought not to be explained away if we seek to understand the reputation of Shakespeare and Jonson in his time.

1671–80

In the eighth decade of the century the allusions to the two poets are more nearly equal than in any other period, except the last: Shakespeare, 173; Jonson, 183. This equality, furthermore, is not a matter of a great spurt in the allusions of one type to counterbalance the usual inequality in others; in most of the common types the distribution is more even than usual. The only exception is the very significant one of allusions calling the poet great, or the greatest of his kind. In this type Jonson holds his usual lead, 43, to 18 for Shakespeare. Thus, in spite of the near equality of the total number of allusions, most of the writers of the decade still acknowledge Jonson's pre-eminence.

In the other types the over-all equality is reflected. There are 39 quotations of Shakespeare to 27 of Jonson. Most of the Shakespearean quotations are found in

---

[12] All the passages in Pepys relating to the drama and theater have been conveniently collected, if not very well discussed, in Miss Helen McAfee's *Pepys on the Restoration Stage* (1916).

commonplace books and anthologies,[13] but most of the Jonson ones are quotations used as illustrations in a connected discourse. There are 48 references to Shakespeare's plays by name and 72 to Jonson's. Shakespeare's characters are alluded to 70 times, Jonson's 68. Even the casual references to the two dramatists by name but without particular significance are about the same—13 to Jonson, 11 to Shakespeare.

As might be expected, more of the allusions in this decade are made by John Dryden than by any other writer. Even Dryden contributed to the even-handed distribution of allusions by referring just 33 times to each dramatist. His great pronouncements of the previous decade probably had much to do with the gradual ascendancy of Shakespeare's reputation, but in this period he shows his preference less clearly.

1681–90

In the decade of the Glorious Revolution the number of allusions falls off somewhat, possibly because of the absorbing character of political events. There are 151 references to Shakespeare and 175 to Jonson. Upon breaking these figures down into types, one finds certain tendencies becoming apparent—tendencies carrying over into the last decade of the century and clearly indicating the rising tide of Shakespeare allusions, which, one would assume, will far surpass the Jonson allusions in the eighteenth century. First, we can notice the principal classes of allusions and then the tendency which they indicate. There are still, in the 1680's, more refer-

[13] The largest group of Shakespeare quotations is provided by the collection called *The New Academy of Compliments* (1671). This volume contains 15 songs from Shakespeare's plays, but I can spot only 2 of Jonson's songs in it.

ences which speak of Jonson as a great poet than of
Shakespeare—37 to 22. The number of quotations from
the two men are about equal—35 passages from Shakespeare and 29 from Jonson. In references to apocryphal
plays, Shakespeare leads, as usual; the 20 Shakespeare
references (mostly from Langbaine) in this class to 2 for
Jonson are a fair index of the larger number of plays in
the Shakespeare apocrypha. The significant change is
seen in the comparative number of allusions to the
plays and the characters of the two playwrights. There
are 120 references to particular plays of Shakespeare as
compared to 137 for Jonson, but 78 character references as compared to Jonson's 26. Of casual unclassi-
fiable references to the two poets, there are 34 to Jonson, 9 to Shakespeare.

Before any conclusions are drawn from these figures,
another set should be noted. In this decade fall the allusions from John Aubrey's *Brief Lives*, a manuscript
which grew from 1669 to 1696. According to my practice, I have considered it in the year which falls midway
between these terminal dates, or 1682. In Aubrey's biographies there are 40 allusions to Jonson, 3 to Shakespeare, including the lives of both the dramatists; that
is, when Aubrey wrote the lives of their contemporaries
and successors, he took occasion to mention Jonson or
his works 39 times, Shakespeare's only twice. In another collection of the period similar in method to
Aubrey's—William Winstanley's *Lives of the Poets*
(1687)—there are 10 allusions to Jonson outside his own
life, 3 to Shakespeare.

These facts about Aubrey and Winstanley's references and the figures on the allusions calling the poet

great are interestingly and, I think, significantly in contrast with those of the allusions to the characters of the
two dramatists. When Aubrey and Winstanley collected material on the lives of great English writers,
scientists, and political figures, they found occasion to
associate these men with Jonson or his works nine times
as often as with Shakespeare. When men like Oldham,
Shadwell, Roscommon, Tate, Gould, Crowne, Lee—to
name a few of them—spoke of the greatest English
poets, they chose Jonson almost twice as often as Shakespeare. Obviously, Jonson was still thought of as the
great English dramatist. Yet when writers—some of these
included—sought an effective illustration from literature, they chose Shakespeare's characters three times as
often as Jonson's.

Since this same situation in regard to characters is
found to an even more marked degree in the next decade, though it had not prevailed in earlier ones, the period 1681–90 apparently marks the beginning of a general
recognition and acknowledgment of Shakespeare's unequaled powers of characterization[14]—a recognition
which to the modern taste seems so natural as to be inevitable. Though in the 1680's Shakespeare's creations were not yet universally known, or Jonson's almost forgotten—as now—the movement toward the
estimate of our day had clearly begun.

1691–1700

The last decade of the century is the only one in which
more Shakespeare than Jonson allusions have been
found, 251 to 244. Though this difference is not great—

[14] See below, pp. 84–86 and 126.

about 50.75–49.25 per cent—and though unnoted Jonson allusions in the numerous unexamined publications of the period would undoubtedly number more than the 7 which this 1.5 per cent represents, nevertheless, the rise of Shakespeare in general critical esteem is clearly evident.

When the allusions in various classifications are compared, the growth of Shakespeare's reputation becomes clearer. Significant is the fact that Jonson, though still called great more often than Shakespeare, leads by only 48 allusions to 34. This is a far cry from Jonson's dominance of the fourth, fifth, and sixth decades of the century in allusions of this type—63 to 10, 28 to 3, 41 to 7. Equally notable is the increased tendency to quote Shakespeare rather than Jonson: 71 quotations to 28. Most striking of all are the allusions to Shakespeare's characters: 352 to 75 for Jonson.

The casual references to the two dramatists are about equal, 31 to Shakespeare, 29 to Jonson. The references to apocryphal plays are mostly to Shakespeare, 28 to 7; but, as noticed before, this figure is not very significant because of the much greater number of apocryphal plays in the Shakespeare canon.

With all this evidence of increased deference to Shakespeare, the serious considerations of England's poetic past generally give Jonson greater attention. Gerard Langbaine's *Account of the English Dramatic Poets* (1691) refers to Jonson 53 times outside the account of his own life, to Shakespeare 44; Wood's *Athenae Oxonienses* (1691–92), 24 times to Jonson, 14 to Shakespeare. The differences here are not so great as in the accounts of Aubrey and Winstanley in the previous decade; nevertheless, the custom of literary historians is still to keep Jonson more constantly in mind than Shakespeare.

UNDATED ALLUSIONS

When all the printed and manuscript allusions of the seventeenth century have been assigned to the decade in which the text was published or in which the manuscript was written, there still remain a number of references in texts which, though clearly seventeenth century, have not so far been dated with sufficient precision to justify their classification in any particular decade. Most of them, of course, come from unprinted manuscripts. These undated allusions have been filed together, and, though they cannot be made to contribute to an understanding of the decade-by-decade development of the dramatists' reputations, they do suggest certain interesting inferences.

There are 68 of these undated references to Jonson, 13 to Shakespeare. Sixty-three of the Jonson allusions and 7 of the Shakespeare are from manuscript commonplace books,[15] a ratio which is most suggestive, for a large number of the commonplace books from which allusions have been reported fall into this undated

---

[15] Actually, the number of Jonson allusions in the undated commonplace books reported is greater than 63, though just how much greater one cannot tell. The uncertainty is caused by the fact that several of the reports on commonplace books say merely "the poems are by Ben Jonson, Carew, &c.," or "there are poems by Ben Jonson on folios. . . . ." According to the principles I have used, each poem constitutes an allusion, but from such indefinite reports I can count only 1 allusion for the volume or 1 for each page cited where nonconsecutive pages are given. Even in the second case one often finds on investigation that there is more than 1 short poem on a page. Thus an unascertainable number of Jonson allusions in these incompletely reported commonplace books remain uncounted.

In the case of the Shakespeare allusions in the commonplace books, there is never any such uncertainty. Passages referring to Shakespeare are reported in detail. Whenever his work is quoted, the precise number of quotations and their length are

group. The incomplete evidence which we have on commonplace books, then, suggests that in these private repositories of gentlemen of literary tastes the preponderance of Jonsonian over Shakespearean selections is about 9 to 1, whereas in the total number of allusions of all kinds in the century it is only about 9 to 7. From these figures we must infer that in the many commonplace books of the century yet unexamined or unreported far more Jonson than Shakespeare allusions will be found—a further reason for thinking that our present figures on quotations do a greater injustice to Jonson than to Shakespeare.[16]

These figures on the undated allusions provide further evidence, it seems to me, for the conclusions already suggested in considering the writings of Pepys, Aubrey, Winstanley, Langbaine, Wood, *et al.*, namely, that Jonson's prestige was greater than Shakespeare's even in the periods in which one dramatist is referred to about as often as the other. For commonplace books display not only the lines the collector likes but the lines he thinks he *ought* to like; they provide occasions not for the casual references to plays and characters which will be widely recognized but for the copying of whole poems or passages from plays which have won the collector's approval. The extant commonplace books show that this approval was bestowed on Jonson far more often than on Shakespeare.

---

given, and often the texts are collated. This great difference in the precision of the reporting of Shakespeare and Jonson allusions in the commonplace books is simply another phase of the misleading picture of the reputations of the two dramatists which we have inevitably acquired (see chap. iii).

[16] See above, pp. 18–21.

The classification of these undated allusions into types is not so illuminating as for the dated allusions, because there are too few to Shakespeare to make the figures for him mean very much. When the Jonson allusions are examined, one is somewhat surprised to note how often his nondramatic verse is quoted. Of course, epigrams, epitaphs, and short lyrics are much more suitable to commonplace books than passages from plays; but, even so, the disproportion is unexpectedly great. In the 64 quotations from his writings, not one comes from his plays, and only 7 from the masques. All the others represent Jonson the nondramatic poet.

CHAPTER V

THE DISTRIBUTION OF ALLUSIONS BY TYPES

IN THE PRECEDING CHAPTER SOME ATTENTION WAS paid to the *kinds* of allusions to Shakespeare and Jonson; but the primary emphasis has been upon chronological distribution. Further knowledge of the comparative reputations of the two great dramatists in the seventeenth century is to be gained, I think, from a more complete classification of the allusions into types. For this purpose twenty-two classes have been set up. These classes are not arbitrary, logical divisions into which all allusions to any author in any time must fall but are the result of a consideration of the 3,269 allusions to Shakespeare and Jonson which have been accepted for this study and of the variety they present. I have tried to devise classes which will reveal most about the terms in which seventeenth-century writers thought of the two poets and their works. A great many of the allusions fall into more than one class—a poem in praise of Shakespeare, for instance, may mention four of his plays and six of his characters and quote three lines; in such a case the allusion is put into several different classes, for it is much more revealing to note the various aspects of Shakespeare's reputation to which the author was contributing than to make an arbitrary decision as to which type is most fully represented. As a consequence of this method of multiple classification,

the total number of allusions by classes—over 5,000—
is much greater than the actual number of separate passages referring to Shakespeare and Jonson. Thus the
total number of allusions by classes is a meaningless
figure, but the number in any one class is significant.

The various classes into which the 3,269 allusions to
both dramatists have been divided follow.

CLASS I

Passages in which the name of the dramatist is used
alone as a standard of poetic or dramatic greatness.

> The World is busie now; and some dare say
> We have not seen of late one good New Play.
> And such believe Shakespear, long since in 's Grave,
> In Choicest Lybraries a place will have
> When not a modern Play will scape the fire.
>
> —NEVIL PAYNE, Epilogue, *The Morning Ramble* (1673)

> As twere the only office of a Friend
> To Rhyme, and 'gainst his Conscience to commend;
> And sweare like Poets of the Post, This Play
> Exceeds all Johnson's Works.
>
> —Commendatory verses by RICHARD WEST, prefixed to
> JAMES FERRAND'S EPΩTOMANIA (1640)[1]

Allusions in Class I are in some ways the most revealing of all, for each one of them specifically desig-
nates Shakespeare or Jonson as a standard of greatness.
In allusions of this type the evidence of Jonson's pre-
eminence in the estimates of the time is overwhelming.
In every single decade of the century he is praised more
often than Shakespeare, and his total is nearly three times
as great (p. 64). The greater reputation of Jonson is most
notable in the fourth, fifth, sixth, and seventh decades
of the century. The figures in these years really repre-

---

[1] For further examples of allusions in this class see Vol. II, pp. 11, 83, and 135.

sent Jonson's early posthumous reputation, for in the
fourth decade, only 11 of 63 allusions offering Jonson
the highest praise were published before his death in
1637. Such a growth in an artist's reputation in the
years immediately following his death is, of course, a
familiar phenomenon. These figures, however, afford
clear evidence that this phenomenon did not occur in
the growth of Shakespeare's reputation.

DISTRIBUTION OF ALLUSIONS

IN CLASS 1

	Shake-speare	Jonson
1601–1610	4	7
1611–1620	2	7
1621–1630	5	8
1631–1640	10	63
1641–1650	3	28
1651–1660	7	41
1661–1670	9	24
1671–1680	18	43
1681–1690	22	37
1691–1700	34	48
Undated	1	0
Totals	115	306

Another noteworthy fact demonstrated by the distribution of these allusions is to be seen in the comparative figures for Shakespeare and for Jonson in the
last two decades of the century. As we have already
noted,[2] these two decades seem to mark the beginning of
the flood tide of Shakespeare's reputation, especially as
seen in quotations from his works and references to his
characters. In the nineties, indeed, the total number of
allusions to Shakespeare for the first time outnumbers
those to Jonson. Yet even in these two decades Jonson
still clearly dominates the field when men of literary
tastes speak of the greatest English dramatist.

[2] See above, pp. 55–57.

CLASS 2

A complete poem or a long passage (exclusive of biographical or bibliographical accounts) devoted wholly to the author or his works. The passage may be elaborate praise, or it may be an extended attack; concentration on Shakespeare or Jonson is the prime distinction. One illustration will suffice, since most of the passages in this class are too long to quote. Familiar examples are those in the front matter of the 1623 Folio or in *Jonsonus Virbius*.

TO THE MEMORY OF BEN JONSON

The Muses fairest light in no dark time;
The wonder of a learned age; the line
Which none can pass; the most proportion'd wit,
To nature, the best judge of what was fit;
The deepest, plainest, highest, clearest pen;
The voice most echo'd by consenting men
The soul which answer'd best to all well said
By others, and which most requital made.
—ANON., *Jonsonus Virbius* (1638)[3]

Allusions of this class are similar in their implication of the subject's reputation to those of Class 1. The composition of an extended passage about Shakespeare or Jonson is in itself evidence of the power of the name, even though the passage be a satiric attack rather than praise. There are more than three times as many allusions of this type to Jonson as to Shakespeare, with an unusual predominance of the Jonson allusions in the first and fourth decades (p. 66). The size of the collection in the first decade is largely accounted for by the numerous long passages about Jonson in Dekker's castigating

[3] The poem may have been written by Sidney Godolphin, since it is found in a manuscript collection of his poems (see John Drinkwater in the *Times Literary Supplement*, October 25, 1923). Other allusions of this class may be found in Vol. II, pp. 45–46, 52–53, 58–59, and 201.

Satiromastix and by the commendatory verses written for the first editions of *Sejanus* and *Volpone*. Twenty-six of the 30 passages come from these three sources. One is again reminded of the importance to Jonson's early reputation of the fact that his caustic tongue inspired articulate enemies and that he supervised careful editions of his plays.

The 5-to-1 predominance of verses on Jonson in the fourth decade is, of course, a result of the great out-

DISTRIBUTION OF ALLUSIONS
IN CLASS 2

	Shake-speare	Jonson
1601–1610..........	1	30
1611–1620..........	4	15
1621–1630..........	12	9
1631–1640..........	15	74
1641–1650..........	2	13
1651–1660..........	3	16
1661–1670..........	0	2
1671–1680..........	1	6
1681–1690..........	5	3
1691–1700..........	6	2
Undated............	5	8
Totals..........	54	178

pouring of praise immediately after his death. About half the verses were printed in *Jonsonus Virbius* in 1638. In no decade of the century is the entire output of poems and long passages about Shakespeare ever half so great as the poems to Jonson in this single volume. Indeed, all the poems to Shakespeare in the first half of the century just about equal the number in *Jonsonus Virbius*, or half the number in the decade of Jonson's death.

It is also noteworthy that the poems and long passages to Shakespeare and Jonson fall off sharply after the Restoration. The passages to the two poets together are fewer in the last four decades than the Jonson allusions alone in the 1630's. It might be informative to collect Dryden allusions of this type in the last four decades and compare their number to the Shakespeare and Jonson ones.

Of the three decades in which Shakespeare allusions of this type outnumber the Jonson ones, the decade of the 1620's is to be explained by the appearance of the verses and prose passages in the Folio of 1623. In the last two decades, though the numbers are small, they may be said to represent the growing tendency to accept Shakespeare as the greatest English dramatist. The figures on allusions of Class 1 are, however, somewhat more conclusive evidence on the status of this movement, since the numbers there are much larger and the praise more uniform.

CLASS 3

The "great triumvirate"—Shakespeare, Jonson, and Beaumont and Fletcher—or any two of them, named as the standard of greatness or as the standard representatives of Elizabethan drama or literature. This type of allusion must be one of the most familiar to readers of all seventeenth-century and particularly Restoration literature. A good example is found in Owen Feltham's poem in *Jonsonus Virbius*:

> And should the Stage compose her selfe a Crowne
> Of all those *wits*, which hitherto sh'as knowne:
> Though there be many that about her brow
> Like sparkling stones, might a quick lustre throw:
> Yet *Shakespeare, Beaumont, Johnson,* these three shall
> Make up the Jem in the point Verticall.

Equally characteristic and somewhat more specific is Edward Phillips' statement in *Theatrum poetarum* (1675):

> *John Fletcher*, one of the happy *Triumvirat* (the other two being *Johnson* and *Shakespear*) of the Chief Dramatic Poets of our Nation, in the last

foregoing Age, among whom there might be said to be a symmetry of perfection, while each excelled in his peculiar way [p. 108].[4]

Since allusions of this class normally name both
Shakespeare and Jonson, there is very little difference
in the numbers for each. Occasionally, however, only
two of the triumvirate, Shakespeare, Jonson, Beaumont
and Fletcher, are named together. Usually when one is
dropped it is Beaumont and Fletcher, especially early in
the century, and only Shakespeare and Jonson are

DISTRIBUTION OF ALLUSIONS
IN CLASS 3

	Shake-speare	Jonson
1601–1610	0	0
1611–1620	0	0
1621–1630	0	1
1631–1640	12	8
1641–1650	13	9
1651–1660	14	16
1661–1670	23	23
1671–1680	37	36
1681–1690	30	30
1691–1700	45	49
Undated	1	0
Totals	175	172

named; but on several occasions it is Shakespeare or
Jonson who is omitted. These figures indicate that Jonson is so dropped somewhat oftener than Shakespeare.

The figures of the frequency of allusions of this sort
reveal practically nothing about the difference between
the reputations of Shakespeare and Jonson. Usually the
allusions do not distinguish among the members of the
triumvirate. The steady increase of such allusions from
decade to decade, except for the eighties, is suggestive of
the growing tendency of writers to think of earlier
English drama as the achievement of Shakespeare, Jonson, and Beaumont and Fletcher.

4 Other examples may be examined in Vol. II, pp. 8–9, 12, and 232.

CLASS 3a

Shakespeare or Jonson and two or three other poets, not of the "triumvirate," named as a standard of greatness. This class is properly a corollary of the foregoing; it has little significance in itself, but it does serve to show how infrequently writers of the seventeenth century named Shakespeare or Jonson in a small group of great poets of the past other than the triumvirate. The class scarcely needs illustration. The most familiar example is William Basse's poem in memory of Shakespeare. Even in this poem it should be noted that Basse's selection of great poets is limited by place of burial and by the fact that Jonson and Fletcher were still alive when he wrote.

> Renowned Spencer lye a thought more nye
> To learned Chaucer, and rare Beaumond lye
> A little neerer Spenser, to make roome
> For Shakespeare in your threefold, fowerfold Tombe.[5]
>
> —Lansdowne MSS 777

The figures on allusions of this class (p. 70) are useful chiefly for comparison with the figures of the preceding class. Such a comparison affords additional evidence that when seventeenth-century writers mentioned great dramatists of the past[6] they generally selected Shake-

---

[5] Among gentlemen of literary tastes in the seventeenth century this poem appears to have been the most popular tribute to Shakespeare. *The Shakspere Allusion-Book* records 10 manuscript and 5 printed examples. Other examples of allusions of this class may be found in Vol. II, pp. 83 and 106–7.

[6] One could almost say "great *poets* of the past," for in most of the allusions of Class 3a the name of Jonson or Shakespeare is coupled not with dramatists but with Chaucer, Spenser, or Sidney. Such a statement is not really warranted, however, for I have not collected the allusions to Chaucer, Spenser, and Sidney which mention neither Shakespeare nor Jonson; I do not know how many examples of such allusions there are. My impression from reading a good part of the literarily allusive passages of the century and from examining but not counting or classifying the collected Chaucer and Spenser allusions is that no group of nondramatic literary names is found half so often as Shakespeare, Jonson, Beaumont and Fletcher.

speare, Jonson, Beaumont and Fletcher, or some two of the trio. Only infrequently did they select one member of the triumvirate to group with two or three others not of the triumvirate—Jonson about one-fourth as often as he was included in the triumvirate, Shakespeare one-eighth as often. Even here the preference for Jonson is unequivocal.

DISTRIBUTION OF ALLUSIONS
IN CLASS 3a

	Shake-speare	Jonson
1601–1610	0	2
1611–1620	0	0
1621–1630	3	3
1631–1640	6	3
1641–1650	2	2
1651–1660	1	6
1661–1670	0	4
1671–1680	0	1
1681–1690	0	7
1691–1700	4	11
Undated	5	0
Totals	21	39

CLASS 4

Shakespeare or Jonson named in a list of literary men, not confined to the triumvirate, but a list in which Shakespeare or Jonson is given particular distinction. Allusions of this and the following class are frequently part of rather extended critical passages, like the As-sizes-on-Parnassus compositions. Often both Shakespeare and Jonson are especially distinguished from the other writers mentioned. When reasons for their distinction are given in passages of this type, Jonson is generally admired for his learning. There seems to be no clear consensus in the assignment of reasons for Shakespeare's distinction.

And finally for Poetrie, 1 *Gower*, 2 Lidgate . . . . 3 the famous *Geofrie Chawcer* . . . . 4 Sir *Philip Sidney* . . . . 5 The renowned Spencer . . . . 6 Sam. Daniel . . . . 7 with Michael Draiton . . . . 8 Beaumount . . . . 9 Fletcher . . . . 10 My friend *Ben Iohnson*, equall to any of the Antients for the exactness of his Pen, and the decorum which he kept in *Dramatick* Poems, never before observed on the *English* Theatre.—PETER HEYLYN, *Cosmographie* (1652), Lib. I, p. 268.

> See how the Learned shades do meet,
> And like Aeriall shadowes fleet,
> More in number than were spide
> To flock 'bout the *Dulichian* Guide.
> The first, *Museus*, then *Catullus*,
> Then *Naso*, *Flaccus*, and *Tibullus;*
> Then *Petrarch*, *Sydney*, none can move
> *Shakespeare* out of Adonis Grove,
> There sullenly he sits.

—Verses by ANTHONY DAVENPORT, prefixed to SAMUEL SHEPPARD'S *Loves of Amandus and Sophronia* (1650)[7]

Allusions of this type, comprising longer lists of great literary figures of the past, are not common early in the century. Probably the most familiar early list—and that too early for this study—is the one Francis Meres set forth in 1598 in his *Palladis Tamia*. Meres's long list of forty or fifty literary names and his undiscriminating praise are fairly characteristic of this type. Such lists are counted as allusions of Class 4 only when Shakespeare or Jonson is given special distinction. The two dramatists are so distinguished about an equal number of times, though Jonson, as usual, leads. The numbers are too small to make the comparison by decades very significant. It is not normal to find twice as many allusions to Jonson as to Shakespeare in the 1680's or to find three times as many allusions to Shakespeare as to Jonson in the 1660's.

[7] Other allusions of this type may be examined in Vol. II, pp. 82–83 and 235.

DISTRIBUTION OF ALLUSIONS
IN CLASS 4

	Shake-speare	Jonson
1601–1610	0	0
1611–1620	0	0
1621–1630	1	0
1631–1640	0	3
1641–1650	3	5
1651–1660	2	6
1661–1670	6	2
1671–1680	1	1
1681–1690	2	4
1691–1700	5	4
Undated	0	0
Totals	20	25

CLASS 5

Shakespeare or Jonson named in a list of three or more literary men, not the triumvirate, and without particular distinction. This class is just the residue of the lists-of-writers allusions after the passages of Classes 3, 3a, and 4 types have been segregated. Probably it does not need illustration, but examples may be found in Volume II, pp. 9, 135, 150, and 215–16.

Allusions of this class differ from those of the former only in that Shakespeare is not particularly distinguished in his lists or Jonson in his—usually nobody is distinguished in such lists. The fact that Jonson is named in half again as many lists as Shakespeare and that in every decade save one he is cited oftener is indicative of Jonson's reputation in nonliterary groups; for such lists, without discrimination among the poets, are usually found in works not primarily concerned with literature, like political histories. Not only did men of developed literary interests—men who talked about the distinctions of particular writers and who quoted from their works—prefer Jonson to Shakespeare in the seventeenth century; but men of less apparent literary interests, men who made a passing statement about literature in a political or social discussion, were also apparently more familiar with Jonson. Again the modern reader is given pause: in more than one-fourth of the seventeenth-century lists of literary men which distinguish or at least mention Jonson, Shakespeare is completely ignored.

DISTRIBUTION OF ALLUSIONS
IN CLASS 5

	Shake-speare	Jonson
1601–1610	3	3
1611–1620	5	6
1621–1630	0	1
1631–1640	1	4
1641–1650	9	10
1651–1660	14	15
1661–1670	5	10
1671–1680	8	9
1681–1690	3	6
1691–1700	7	19
Undated	0	0
Totals	55	83

The numbers of allusions of this class taken by decades are again somewhat too small for illuminating comparison. The large number of lists-with-Jonson as compared to lists-with-Shakespeare in the last decade is not characteristic.

CLASS 6

Quotations from the works of Shakespeare or Jonson with or without acknowledgment as illustration or authority, i.e., quotations intended to be read in their context. This is the first of three classes of quotations, distinguished from the other two in that the Shakespearean or Jonsonian lines are frankly quoted, but not simply for their own sakes as in an anthology or commonplace book. Quotations of this type in the seventeenth century are more often from classic than from English authors, especially those intended not simply to illustrate but to exercise the weight of authority.

Loyal all over! except one Knave, which I hope no body will take to himself; or if he do, I must e'en say with *Hamlet*,
.... *Then let the strucken Deer go weep.* ....
— APHRA BEHN, *The City-Heiress* (1682),
the Epistle Dedicatory

And for my greater Authority I will adde these few excellent Verses of our Famous *Johnson* on this subject, which he calls a fit Rhime against Rhime.
Rhime the rack of finest Wits
. . . .
And as I doubt not well enough to wave any oblique exception that any man can throw on my Opinion (since patronized by his) so I do not detract from the deserts of any..... — EDWARD HOWARD, Preface to *The Womens Conquest* (1671).[8]

These allusions are frankly quotations, though the author of them may not be named, and they are intended to impress the reader with their aptness or the weight of their authority. It is the second class so far noted in which the Shakespeare allusions outnumber the Jonson ones.

The greater Shakespearean total is due to the situation in the first three decades and the tenth. In the other six decades the numbers are about even: 56 quotations from Shakespeare, 61 from Jonson. In the first two decades the difference is evidently due to the earlier publication dates of Shakespeare's works, for 6 of the 8 quotations are from plays and poems of Shakespeare published in the sixteenth century before anything of

[8] Other examples of allusions in this class may be found in Vol. II, pp. 136, 228, and 254.

Jonson's was in print.[9] The other 2 quotations are from *Hamlet*, 1603 and 1604.

The situation in the last decade is the clearest example we have had so far of the evident rise of Shakespeare's reputation in the closing years of the century. For the first time in any decade in any class in which the numbers are large enough to have much meaning, the Shakespearean allusions are more than twice as numerous as the Jonsonian ones. This class is, further-

DISTRIBUTION OF ALLUSIONS
IN CLASS 6

	Shake-speare	Jonson
1601–1610	3	0
1611–1620	5	0
1621–1630	9	2
1631–1640	3	3
1641–1650	9	1
1651–1660	2	5
1661–1670	5	6
1671–1680	10	18
1681–1690	27	28
1691–1700	70	30
Undated	0	0
Totals	143	93

more, a significant one, for acknowledged quotations (as opposed to plagiarism) from an author are fairly good indications that his name or his lines can be expected to receive a respectful hearing. The first clear indications of anything like a general recognition of the unsurpassed quotableness of Shakespeare's lines is afforded by the figures for this decade. One would surmise that the number of Shakespearean quotations continued steadily to increase from the 1690's to the end of the nineteenth century.[10]

[9] *Venus and Adonis, Richard III, Romeo and Juliet.*

[10] The 1939 edition of Bartlett's *Familiar Quotations* has 1,849 quotations from Shakespeare, 41 from Jonson.

CLASS 7

Quotations of one or more lines from the works of Shakespeare or Jonson or quotations of passages about them or independent transcripts of their works, in commonplace books, anthologies, and independent manuscripts; sometimes the author is identified and sometimes not. Passages in this class, unlike those in Class 6, have little or no relation to their context. At most, they

DISTRIBUTION OF ALLUSIONS
IN CLASS 7

	Shake-speare	Jonson
1601–1610	2	16
1611–1620	1	7
1621–1630	0	40
1631–1640	11	18
1641–1650	16	36
1651–1660	172	147
1661–1670	1	4
1671–1680	25	8
1681–1690	1	0
1691–1700	1	4
Undated	0	64
Totals	230	344

appear in a section of an anthology devoted to a particular theme; generally they would be equally appropriate if moved several pages backward or forward in the manuscript or book in which they occur. Allusions of this type are quite numerous, but they require no illustration.[11]

About nine-tenths of the allusions in this class come from commonplace books and printed anthologies, in which they have no relation to their context. At first glance it seems unaccountable that Jonson should lead in this class by an even larger number than Shakespeare

---

[11] Examples are printed in Vol. II, pp. 2–3, 38–40, and 142.

did in the similar Class 6. The explanation seems to be that a large number of these allusions—perhaps one-third—come from manuscript sources, especially commonplace books, and Jonson is overwhelmingly dominant in such sources. Every one of the allusions in the undated group comes from a manuscript, and there the Jonson domination is greater than at any other point in the entire study. The extant seventeenth-century manuscript commonplace books are largely the products of the pens of undergraduates at Oxford and Cambridge, college dons, and gentlemen of leisure; with these groups Jonson seems, throughout the century, to have been held in far greater respect than Shakespeare. Jonson's name and copies of his poems—often copies of several poems—are usually to be found in such books, Shakespeare's seldom. Though I have not separated all the manuscript allusions in this class from the printed ones, my impression is that of the printed allusions a few more quote Shakespeare than Jonson. In the manuscript sources, quotations from Jonson are usually acknowledged, quotations from Shakespeare usually are not.

This discrepancy between printed and manuscript allusions to Shakespeare and Jonson is rather challenging. To what extent is Shakespeare's rising reputation in the late seventeenth century due to social changes? To what extent is Shakespeare's reputation a London reputation and Jonson's an Oxford and Cambridge one? Had the introduction of printing into England been delayed two hundred years, what would the comparative bulk of extant Shakespeare and Jonson works have been, and what would their comparative reputations have been today?

CLASS 8

Quotations of one or more lines from the works of Shakespeare or Jonson lifted without acknowledgment. Allusions in this class, like those in Class 6, depend on their context, but they are not acknowledged, and they are not cited to bring to bear the weight of authority. Sometimes they are simple examples of plagiarism, but more often they are intended as burlesques of the original.

WIFE: . . . . Hold up thy head, Ralph; show the gentlemen what thou canst do; speak a huffing part; I warrant you the gentlemen will accept of it.

CIT: Do, Ralph, do.

RALPH: By heaven, methinks, it were an easy leap
To pluck bright honor from the pale-faced moon;
Or dive into the bottom of the sea,
Where never fathom-line touched any ground,
And pluck up drowned honor from the lake of hell.
—BEAUMONT and FLETCHER, Induction, *The Knight
of the Burning Pestle* (1613)

How I shall hurle *Protesebastus'* panting brain
Into the Air in mites as small as Atomes.
—ANON., *The Unfortunate Usurper* (1663), I, 4[12]

In the recorded examples of this type of allusion, Shakespeare is clearly dominant; in only one decade are the quotations from Jonson more numerous. One hesitates, however, to be too sure of the evidence; for the completeness of the collection in this type is more doubtful than in any other. The recognition of such allusions as these depends wholly upon familiarity with the lines of Shakespeare and Jonson, for there is generally no sign of allusion except the quoted words themselves. This is precisely the area in which the Jonson-compe-

---

[12] The lines are Jonson's (*Sejanus*, I, 256–57, with "Protesebastus" substituted for "his"). Other examples will be found in Vol. II, pp. 13, 29, and 41–42.

tence of all investigators is most inferior to their Shake-speare-competence.[13] Probably very few lines quoted from Shakespeare in accessible texts are still undetected; hundreds of lines from Jonson may be. Thus, in spite of our modern feeling that Shakespeare's lines *must* have impressed themselves on the minds of his contemporaries far more than Jonson's, we cannot be sure of the facts. Such evidence as we have confirms the modern assumption.

DISTRIBUTION OF ALLUSIONS
IN CLASS 8

	Shake-speare	Jonson
1601–1610	5	0
1611–1620	3	1
1621–1630	0	1
1631–1640	8	1
1641–1650	6	2
1651–1660	1	1
1661–1670	0	3
1671–1680	4	1
1681–1690	7	1
1691–1700	0	0
Undated	0	0
Totals	34	11

The total number of allusions in this group is small, but it should be pointed out that this class has probably suffered more from my rejection of dubious parallel passages in the Shakespeare and Jonson allusion books than any other. I have said that an alleged parallel passage is not an allusion unless one full line is quoted.[14] While this test seems to me the best that can be applied to parallel passages, it is, nevertheless, quite possible that in various instances some seventeenth-century writer may have had Shakespeare or Jonson clearly in mind though he lifted less than one line. Such plagiarism,

[13] See above, pp. 20–21.   [14] See above, pp. 8–11.

which to my mind is too uncertain to try to deal with, would fall into this class.

<h2 style="text-align:center">CLASS 9</h2>

Shakespeare's or Jonson's name connected with an apocryphal play, on the title-page, in an advertisement, or in any passage in which the name of the dramatist and a play outside the accepted canon are associated. Allusions of this type scarcely need illustration.

DISTRIBUTION OF ALLUSIONS
IN CLASS 9

	Shake-speare	Jonson
1601–1610	5	0
1611–1620	0	0
1621–1630	1	0
1631–1640	0	0
1641–1650	0	0
1651–1660	16	5
1661–1670	10	0
1671–1680	0	1
1681–1690	20	2
1691–1700	28	7
Undated	0	1
Totals	80	16

The comparative numbers of these allusions to apocryphal plays is a direct reflection of the state of the text and canon of Shakespeare and Jonson. The great majority of the allusions come from title-pages, advertisements, and bibliographies published by such men as Winstanley, Langbaine, and Gildon, so that the ratio of the allusions is close to the ratio of plays in the Shakespeare apocrypha to plays in the Jonson apocrypha. There are about ten plays which are added to the Shakespeare canon by several different bibliographers, and only one so added to the Jonson canon. Ten other plays are erroneously ascribed to Shakespeare by only one man or occasionally by two; only one to Jonson. These ratios are reflected in the numbers of allusions; very few of the references could be called literary allusions.

Shakespeare's notorious unconcern with his published text led inevitably to a swollen apocrypha. Jonson's equally notorious concern with the printing of his plays discouraged unauthorized additions to the canon.

The decades in which most allusions of this type appear are the decades of publishers' and bibliographers' activity. In the first decade of the century Shakespeare's name appears on the title-pages of several plays which, according to general agreement, he did not write. In the sixth and seventh decades the long publishers' lists like those of Archer and Rogers and Ley attribute apocryphal plays to him. In the ninth and tenth decades the bibliographers discuss the apocryphal plays along with the canonical ones. The only apocryphal plays which are connected with the names of Shakespeare or Jonson more than once outside these publishers' and bibliographers' records are *Sir John Oldcastle* and *The Widow*. They alone have left evidence that in the popular mind they were connected with the names of the dramatists to whom they were erroneously attributed.

CLASS 10

References to plays or poems or masques of Shakespeare's or Jonson's by name or unmistakable synopsis. Every sort of mention of such a work is counted in this class.

BOWDLER: I never read anything but *Venus and Adonis.*
CRIPPLE: Why thats the very quintessence of love,
 If you remember but a verse or two,
 Ile pawne my head, goods, lands, and all 'twill doe.

—THOMAS HEYWOOD, *The Fair Maid
 of the Exchange* (1607), sig. G₃

An *Alchymist* vsually answers his deluded scholler with expectation of
Proiection, and tells him the more his *Materials* be multiplied, the stronger
will the *Proiection* be; especially if it come to the mountenance of an hundred pounds, *Vid.* The Play of the *Alchymist.*—JOHN GEE, *New Shreds of
the Old Snare* (1624), p. 22 n.[15]

DISTRIBUTION OF ALLUSIONS
IN CLASS 10

	Shake-speare	Jonson
1601–1610	32	29
1611–1620	30	20
1621–1630	18	19
1631–1640	27	62
1641–1650	12	36
1651–1660	25	41
1661–1670	60	137
1671–1680	48	72
1681–1690	120	137
1691–1700	192	208
Undated	3	6
Totals	567	767

The next three classes are concerned with allusions to
works and characters. Class 10 includes all specific references to any play, poem, or masque in the accepted
Shakespeare or Jonson canon. Each name is recorded
separately; thus, if a writer commends 5 tragedies of
Shakespeare, the passage is counted as 5 examples of
Class 10, but counted as only 1 allusion in the total
count. Sometimes, particularly in the eighties and nine-

[15] Other examples of the type will be found in Vol. II, pp. 87, 147, and 203–5.

ties, a single long allusion of a biographical or critical character will contain 40 or more allusions of Class 10. This fact should be kept in mind in considering allusions of Classes 10, 11, 11a, 12, and 13. The numbers are large because every mention of a play, masque, or poem by name is counted under Class 10, regardless of the other classes into which the allusion may fall.

The comparative figures here are somewhat misleading; actually, the dominance of Jonson is greater than it appears, because the number of plays in the Shakespeare canon is greater than that in the Jonson. For instance, in his account of Shakespeare, Winstanley lists 48 works, several apocryphal, of course, while his equally laudatory account of Jonson lists only 21. Winstanley does not really speak of Shakespeare's plays twice as often as he does of Jonson's, as the figures alone would imply. In fact, outside the biographies of the two men, he refers to Jonson 10 times, to Shakespeare only 3 times.

This difference in the size of the canon is responsible for the greater number of allusions to Shakespeare in the first and second decades. By the end of 1610 there were at least thirty-five Shakespearean works in existence to refer to, but not more than thirteen Jonsonian, excluding the masques. In every other decade of the century the allusions to Jonson's works by name are more numerous, in spite of the larger Shakespeare canon.

The character of the allusions to Jonson's masques presents another factor to be considered in comparing these figures. In the first and second decades of the century they are more frequently mentioned than the plays;[16] yet, since they are seldom referred to by name, very few of the allusions to them are counted in this class.[17] These factors—the size of the Shakespeare canon and the namelessness of Jonson's masques—make the comparative familiarity of Shakespeare's titles appear greater than it really was.

This specific preference of seventeenth-century writers for Jonson's plays over Shakespeare's as shown, though inadequately, by the table for Class 10 is perhaps even more shocking to the modern taste than the general praise of Jonson over Shakespeare. It is not too difficult to understand that to the critical and literary mind of the seventeenth century Jonson's learning and his superb structural skill might in the abstract have seemed more admirable than Shakespeare's lyric eloquence and matchless characterization. But when it came down to specific cases, did these seventeenth-century writers actually prefer *Volpone* and *Sejanus* and *Catiline* to *As You Like It* and *Macbeth* and *King Lear?* The figures indicate that they did, and the later figures on allusions to individual plays exhibit the preference beyond the shadow of a doubt. *O tempora! O mores!*

CLASS 11

Literary references to a character in the works of Shakespeare or Jonson. Such references are generally for purposes of illustration, and almost always the character is mentioned by name, though occasionally there is an unmistakable allusion of this type when no name is mentioned.

[16] See above, pp. 38–40.

[17] See below, pp. 87–88, 90–91, 109.

Our Keepers knew no hurt, unlesse 't had bin
Drinking of Sack, honest *Iack Falstaffes* sinne.

—B. R., *The Cambridge Royallist Imprisoned*
(July 31, 1643), sig. A₄

Thay Quakte at Iohnson as by hym thay pase
because of Trebulation Holsome and Annanias.

—G. C. Moore Smith (ed.), *William Hemminge's El-
egy on Randolph's Finger* (1923), lines 183–84[18]

DISTRIBUTION OF ALLUSIONS
IN CLASS 11

	Shake-speare	Jonson
1601–1610	14	9
1611–1620	9	31
1621–1630	14	12
1631–1640	21	20
1641–1650	30	2
1651–1660	40	39
1661–1670	48	44
1671–1680	67	67
1681–1690	78	26
1691–1700	341	70
Undated	34	0
Totals	696	320

The references to characters present an aspect of Shakespeare's and Jonson's reputations more like the modern situation than any other revealed in this classification of allusions. In every decade except the second and eighth, Shakespeare's characters seem better known. Again it is well to remember that Shakespeare created several times as many characters as Jonson did, not only because he wrote twice as many plays, but because his normal cast is about twice the size of Jonson's. This fact does not, however, wholly account for the difference, for Shakespeare's twenty most familiar char-

---

[18] This type of allusion is one of the commonest. There are many examples in Vol. II, a few of which will be found on pp. 2, 6, 135, and 203–5.

acters are mentioned nearly three times as often as Jonson's twenty most familiar.[19] Though writers of the seventeenth century praised Jonson more than Shakespeare, though they discussed him oftener, quoted him oftener, mentioned his plays oftener, and recorded more performances of his works, they were evidently more deeply impressed by Shakespeare's characterizations than by Jonson's. This particular aspect of Shakespeare's creative genius triumphed over the critical standards which generally blinded the men of his time to his superiority.

CLASS 11*a*

References to characters of Shakespeare or Jonson as acting roles. Such theatrical allusions are much less common than the literary ones; but they are of no little importance, for they furnish highly desirable but generally inaccessible data on the plays of Shakespeare and Jonson in the environment for which they were intended— the theater.

Decemb. 3. 1662.

. . . . only the other day, when Othello was play'd, the Doge of Venice and all his Senators came upon the Stage with Feathers in their Hats, which was like to have chang'd the Tragedy into a Comedy, but that the Moor and Desdemona acted their Parts well.[20]—CATHERINE PHILIPS, *Letters from Orinda to Paliarchus* (1705), p. 96.

April 17th [1669]

. . . . and there hearing that "The Alchymist" was acted, we did go, and took him with us to the King's house; and it is still a good play, having not been acted for two or three years before; but I do miss Clun, for the Doctor.—H. B. WHEATLEY (ed.), *The Diary of Samuel Pepys.*[21]

[19] See the analysis of allusions to particular characters below, pp. 120 ff.

[20] This is a good example of an allusion which is classified in two different groups; it is both 11*a* and 12.

[21] Other allusions of this type will be found in Vol. II, pp. 13, 14, and 109.

Though the number of allusions in this class is too small to be wholly reliable, there is little doubt that Shakespeare's acting roles made more of an impression in the theater than Jonson's, as one would expect from the greater familiarity of his characters as revealed by the allusions in the preceding class. It is not surprising that three-fourths of these references to acting roles

DISTRIBUTION OF ALLUSIONS
IN CLASS 11a

	Shake-speare	Jonson
1601–1610.	4	0
1611–1620.	3	0
1621–1630.	0	0
1631–1640.	0	0
1641–1650.	0	0
1651–1660.	3	0
1661–1670.	12	3
1671–1680.	3	1
1681–1690.	0	0
1691–1700.	11	5
Undated.	1	0
Totals.	37	9

come from the last four decades of the century, for one of the most exasperating aspects of the study of the great Elizabethan dramatic outburst is the paucity of literary references to the plays in the theatrical environment for which they were written. Even when Jonson's friends refer to the fate of his plays in the theater, as in the commendatory verses for *Sejanus* and *Volpone*, they seldom say anything specific about the performance of particular roles.

CLASS 12

Literary or social references to performances or preparations for performances of plays or masques by Shakespeare or Jonson. Theatrical allusions of this type are nearly always made by members of the audience, or potential members of the audience; they are distinguished from passages of the following type which are nearly always made by, or in dealings with, members of the producing group.

1635, May 6.
 not farre from home all day att the bla: ffryers & a play this day Called the More of Venice.—"The Records of Sir Humphrey Mildmay," *The Jacobean and Caroline Stage*, II, 677.

The Masque [Jonson's *Masque of Beauty*] was as well performed as ever any was; and for the device of it, with the Speeches and Verses, I had sent it your Lordship ere this, if I could have gotten those of Ben Jonson. But no sooner had he made an end of these, but that he undertook a new charge for the Masque [*Lord Hadington's Masque* or *The Hue and Cry after Cupid*] that is to be at the Viscount Hadington's Mariage.[22]—Rowland Whyte to the Earl of Shrewsbury, January 29,1607/8, in J. B. NICHOLS, *The Progresses of James the First* (1828), II, 175.[23]

At first glance the dominance of Jonson in allusions of this class seems a contradiction of the evidence of Class 11*a* concerning the comparative familiarity of the acting roles of the two dramatists. Two facts largely explain the discrepancy. First, most of the allusions in the first and second decades refer to the performances of masques, and the characters in the masques are almost never mentioned in allusions of any type. In the masque performances the spectacle completely overshadowed the characters; on the few occasions when actors were mentioned, they were referred to for social and not for

 [22] Whyte's statement is a good example of a single passage which constitutes two separate allusions, for he records both the performance of one masque and the preparation for another. Note that, as usual, though both masques are clearly indicated, neither is actually named.

 [23] Other examples of allusions of this type will be found in Vol. II, pp. 22–24, 34, and 115.

DISTRIBUTION OF ALLUSIONS
IN CLASS 12

	Shake-speare	Jonson
1601–1610	10	27
1611–1620	9	29
1621–1630	2	8
1631–1640	1	7
1641–1650	0	0
1651–1660	3	12
1661–1670	41	43
1671–1680	3	3
1681–1690	1	0
1691–1700	5	5
Undated	0	0
Totals	75	134

theatrical reasons. The second relevant fact is the customary attitude toward Shakespeare and Jonson in the seventeenth-century theater. Shakespeare's plays were generally thought of as acting vehicles, Jonson's as presentations of the work of a master; in the former, acting roles are a relevant and important consideration, in the latter they are not. Pepys's remarks, as noted in chapter iv, clearly reveal this attitude.[24] An even more compelling illustration is the frequent revision and adaptation of Shakespeare's plays for the Restoration stage as compared with the fidelity to Jonson's own text. The frequent cries of pedantic anguish uttered by modern writers over the mutilation of Shakespeare's text in the "improved" Restoration versions of his plays, the indignant protests against the "vandalism" of Davenant, Dryden, Tate, and Crowne, reveal a singularly naïve attitude. These men were not vandals; they were intelligent men of the theater acting in accord with the tastes of the time and the standards of the theater, acting as William Shakespeare himself had acted in his

[24] See above, pp. 49–54.

own theater. He might have been puzzled or even annoyed at the new taste, but he would scarcely have attacked the competent dramatists who were trying to adapt the available material to meet it.

These allusions of Class 12, then, as compared with those of Classes 11 and 11*a*, are an interesting further example of the characteristic seventeenth-century way of viewing Shakespeare and Jonson. The chronological distribution of the allusions is notable chiefly as evidence of the great interest in Jonson's masques in the reign of James I and of the great eagerness with which performances were discussed in the first decade after the reopening of the theaters at the Restoration.

CLASS 13

Business records of performances of, or preparations for performances of, plays or masques by Shakespeare or Jonson.

Playes for the Kinge this present yeare of o^r Lord God. 1630
   At

[H]ampton Court   The 17 of October. Midsomers Night's Dreame
. . . .

—MS 2068.8, Folger Shakespeare Library, printed in
The Jacobean and Caroline Stage, I, 27

The bill of account of the hole charges of the Queen's
Ma^{ts} Maske at Chrismas 1610 [*Love Freed from Ignorance and Folly*]
Inprimis, to Mr. Inigo Johnes, as apeareth by his byll . . 238 li. 16 s. 10 d.
. . . .

Item, for 3 yeardes of flesh collored satten for Cupides
   coate and hose att 14s. the yeard. . . . . 2 li. 2 s.
. . . .

Rewardes to the persons imployed in the maske.
Inprimis, to Mr. Benjamin Johnson for his inventions. . 40 li.
. . . .

Item, to Mr. Johnson for setting the songes to the lutes   5 li.
Item, to Thomas Lupo for setting the dances to the vio-
lens..   5 li.

—Exchequer Papers, printed in *Proceedings of the Society
of Antiquaries of London* (1859–61), Ser. 2, I, 31–32[25]

DISTRIBUTION OF ALLUSIONS
IN CLASS 13

	Shakespeare	Jonson
1601–1610..........	0	10
1611–1620..........	11	17
1621–1630..........	6	8
1631–1640..........	9	10
1641–1650..........	0	0
1651–1660..........	3	2
1661–1670..........	7	21
1671–1680..........	1	6
1681–1690..........	0	1
1691–1700..........	0	3
Undated............	0	0
Totals..........	37	78

The figures on these business records of performances of Shakespeare's and Jonson's plays might be taken as an indication that Jonson was performed oftener in the seventeenth century than Shakespeare. I doubt if this was true; but in any case these figures can scarcely be accepted as evidence on the frequency of performance in the commercial theaters. Nearly two-thirds of the allusions are dated before the closing of the theaters, and allusions of this type in that period nearly all concern court performances of plays or masques. Jonson's greater attraction for courtly audiences, particularly in the masque, is common knowledge; and these figures only

[25] For other examples of allusions of this type see Vol. II, pp. 43, 119, and 137–38.

verify the conclusion suggested by other types of allusions.

After the Restoration, the records of performances in the public theaters are about equal for Shakespeare and Jonson, but Jonson again dominates in the allusions to performances at court. In considering these Restoration records it should be remembered that the most familiar collection of allusions of this type—Downes, *Roscius Anglicanus*—is ruled out because of its date of publication.

CLASS 14

Letters written to Shakespeare or Jonson. Though there are no known allusions of this type to Shakespeare in the seventeenth century, there are several to Jonson.[26]

DISTRIBUTION OF ALLUSIONS
IN CLASS 14

	Shake-speare	Jonson
1601–1610	0	0
1611–1620	0	7
1621–1630	0	5
1631–1640	0	3
1641–1650	0	1
1651–1660	0	0
1661–1670	0	0
1671–1680	0	0
1681–1690	0	0
1691–1700	0	0
Undated	0	1
Totals	0	17

The figures on allusions of this type simply underscore the fulness of our biographical knowledge of Jonson and the scantiness of our knowledge of Shakespeare. But this familiar situation is in itself a manifestation of

[26] Allusions of this class scarcely need illustration; examples may be found in Vol. II, pp. 26–27 and 30–31.

the contemporary reputations of the two men. It is not simply Jonson's intercourse with courtly and learned groups or the later span of his life, important though they are, which have preserved for us our fuller knowledge of him. Jonson's contemporaries, as the above figures show, thought it important or interesting to preserve relics of him; Shakespeare's apparently did not. This fact is in itself a direct reflection of the higher repute in which Jonson was generally held.[27] It should be further noted that these allusions nearly all come from manuscript collections—a type of source in which Shakespeare is generally completely overshadowed by Jonson.

CLASS 15

Records of honors conferred on or proposed for Shakespeare or Jonson. Again there are no examples of allusions to Shakespeare of this type in the seventeenth century, but there are several to Jonson.

Precept	Vigesimo quinto Septembris J^m vj^e Decimo Oc-

Precept
Gild
Jonsoun burges
and gildbrother

Vigesimo quinto Septembris J^m vj^e Decimo Octauo. Ordanis the Deyne of gild to mak Benjamyn Jonsoun inglisman burges and gildbrother in communi forma.

—Edinburgh Council Register, Vol. XIII, fol. 39, in HERFORD and SIMPSON, *Ben Jonson*, I, 233

19 July 1619

Johnson, Benjamin; "omni humana litteratura feliciter instructus et eo nominea serenissimo rege annua pensione eaque satis honorifica honestatus."—ANDREW CLARK (ed.), *Register of the University of Oxford, 1571–1622* (1887), II, 238.[28]

[27] The extant letters to or about Shakespeare are sixteenth-century documents and therefore not considered here (see E. K. Chambers, *William Shakespeare* [Oxford, 1930], II, 101-6). Even these letters are business rather than personal or literary documents, and they appear to have been preserved for economic reasons.

[28] Other examples will be found in Vol. II, pp. 28 and 33.

Though allusions of this type are not the same as those of the former, their implication is similar—the preservation of such records implies a greater concern for Jonson than for Shakespeare. The records themselves, however, imply a much greater contemporary reputation than mere letters do. The records of the nomination of Jonson for Bolton's Royal Academy, of his royal pen-

DISTRIBUTION OF ALLUSIONS
IN CLASS 15

	Shake-speare	Jonson
1601–1610	0	1
1611–1620	0	8
1621–1630	0	8
1631–1640	0	1
1641–1650	0	0
1651–1660	0	0
1661–1670	0	1
1671–1680	0	1
1681–1690	0	0
1691–1700	0	1
Undated	0	0
Totals	0	21

sion, of his appointment as City Chronologer, of his honors at the hands of the Council of the City of Edinburgh, of his honorary degree at Oxford, are all distinctions which not only are not recorded for Shakespeare but which, so far as we can tell, never would have been proposed for him. In our day of the wholesale distribution of honors—academic, civic, and national—no one needs to be reminded that the award of formal honors is not necessarily any proof of solid merit; but such awards in any time are clear evidence of popular reputation—deserved or undeserved.

CLASS 16

Biographical accounts of Shakespeare or Jonson. Most such accounts are too long for illustration here, but the biographical remarks about Shakespeare made by Edward Phillips in 1675 and by Charles Gildon in 1698 are typical and too familiar to require reprinting.[29]

DISTRIBUTION OF ALLUSIONS
IN CLASS 16

	Shake-speare	Jonson
1601–1610	o	o
1611–1620	o	1
1621–1630	o	o
1631–1640	o	o
1641–1650	o	o
1651–1660	o	1
1661–1670	3	1
1671–1680	o	1
1681–1690	4	3
1691–1700	4	4
Undated	o	o
Totals	11	11

The comparative number of allusions of this type is not very revealing, for most of the references come from collections of biographies like Fuller's *Worthies*, Winstanley's *Lives of the Most Famous English Poets*, and Aubrey's *Brief Lives*, which treat both Shakespeare and Jonson, as well as many of their contemporaries. A few come from collections of manuscript notes, like those of Fulman or the Reverend John Ward, and record facts about only one of the two poets. Such collections are really more like commonplace books than like the other dictionaries of biography; their Jonson material is likely to consist of anecdotes—which fall into the next class— while their Shakespeare material is sometimes a fragmentary biography, recorded, apparently, because the information was thought to be curious or out of the way.

[29] Examples of such accounts of Jonson will be found in *The Jonson Allusion-Book*, pp. 112–15 and 354–58.

Personal anecdotes or records of Shakespeare or Jonson. Allusions of this type differ from those in Class 16 in that they make no pretense of biographical or bibliographical completeness.

m^r Ben: Johnson and m^r. W^m: Shake-speare Being Merrye att a Tauern, m^r Jonson haueing begune this for his Epitaph

Here lies Ben Johnson that was once one

he gives ytt to m^r Shakspear to make vpp who presently wrightes

Who while hee liu'de was a sloe things
and now being dead is Nothinge.

finis

—Bodleian Ashmolean MS 38, p. 181, printed in E. K. CHAMBERS, *William Shakespeare*, II, 246

Beniaminu) Johnson Ste
Anne in blackfriers
321.b 1

Presented that he is by fame a seducer of youthe to popishe religion/he was monished to appeare to see farther pceding herin he having denyed bothe the fact & the fame and the Church Wardens weare decreed to be here to specifie what pticulers they have to Charrdg him wth continuat in hunc diem/

—*A Book of Correction, etc.*, Wednesday, May 14, 1606, printed in HERFORD and SIMPSON, *Ben Jonson*, I, 222[30]

Since allusions of this type record both documented fact and popular stories, their numbers bear witness to the greater fulness of biographical source material on Jonson and to the fund of popular anecdotes about him as well. Though there are more Jonson allusions of this class in every decade except the second, the figures are really misleading, for Jonson's dominance is much greater than the figures show. The Shakespeare allusions mostly occur before 1620, three-fourths of them falling in the first two decades. These 50 allusions nearly all concern business transactions or births, deaths, and

[30] Other examples of allusions of this class will be found in Vol. II, pp. 29, 59, 120, and 226.

marriages, and all but 8 or 10 are products of the tireless search for Shakespeare records of any kind in the last seventy-five years. Such records, of course, have nothing to do with Shakespeare's literary reputation, for they were not cherished because of his distinction but merely preserved as legal records. A similar search for Jonson records in the parish registers, at Somerset House, the Public Records Office, and other record

DISTRIBUTION OF ALLUSIONS
IN CLASS 17

	Shake-speare	Jonson
1601–1610	17	24
1611–1620	33	11
1621–1630	2	10
1631–1640	2	13
1641–1650	3	4
1651–1660	4	16
1661–1670	1	12
1671–1680	0	1
1681–1690	2	10
1691–1700	4	9
Undated	1	0
Totals	69	110

repositories would probably turn up as many such Jonson allusions, though of a somewhat different type. If we discounted the allusions of this type to either Jonson or Shakespeare turned up by modern research in record repositories during the last seventy-five years, the Jonson allusions would outnumber the Shakespeare ones 3 or 4 to 1.

Perhaps the anecdotes in this class should have been distinguished from the biographical records, since the two offer different implications about the reputation of their subject. There are, of course, far more anecdotes about Jonson than about Shakespeare. Indeed, the most popular of the Shakespeare anecdotes is one which couples him with Jonson.[31] This greater fund of recorded anecdote about Jonson is to be attributed not alone to the greater interest in him in the century but to the strongly marked character of the man which led to the accretion of stories. The majority of the anecdotes about Jonson concern his drinking, his association with the Tribe of Ben, and his verbal encounters with his contemporaries. The impression of Jonson's bluff pugnacity is witnessed by the epithet which is most frequently applied to him: "honest Ben."

CLASS 18

Casual references to Shakespeare or Jonson in statements not primarily about the dramatist. Allusions of this type never involve praise of the author but sometimes imply unfavorable criticism. Often they are found in accounts of other dramatists in which Shakespeare or Jonson is merely mentioned as a contemporary.

He . . . . in a short time fitted him for the life of a Stage-player in a common society, from whence after venting his frothy inventions, he had a greater call to a higher promotion; namely to be the Jester, (or rather a Fool) in *Shakespears* Company of Players: *Omne simile est appetibile sui similis*, every like desires his like: There he so long sported himself with his own deceivings, till at last like an Infidel Jew, he conceived preaching to be but foolishness.—WILLIAM YONGE, *Englands Shame: . . . . Being a Full and Faithful Relation of the Life and Death of that Grand Imposter Hugh Peters* (1663), pp. 7–8.

November 17, 1621. . . . . Dr. Donne is to be Dean of St. Paul's, so that if Ben Jonson could be Dean of Westminster, St. Paul's, Westminster and Christchurch would each have a poetical Dean.—JOHN CHAMBERLAIN to SIR DUDLEY CARLETON, *Calendar of State Papers, Domestic, James I* (1621), p. 310.[32]

[31] See Vol. II, p. 101, for one of the several examples of this anecdote.

[32] Other allusions of this type may be found in Vol. II, pp. 6, 176, and 208.

This class is really the miscellaneous one into which allusions find their way if they do not properly belong in any of the others. The references say nothing significant about Shakespeare or Jonson; they merely use the names, frequently for purposes of identification. As

DISTRIBUTION OF ALLUSIONS
IN CLASS 18

	Shake-speare	Jonson
1601–1610	2	4
1611–1620	0	3
1621–1630	0	4
1631–1640	6	7
1641–1650	5	7
1651–1660	11	22
1661–1670	6	15
1671–1680	11	13
1681–1690	9	34
1691–1700	31	29
Undated	1	0
Totals	82	138

might be expected, there are more such casual references to Jonson than to Shakespeare in every decade of the century except the last. Though the individual allusions of this class are not important, their sums offer another good index of the popular familiarity of Shakespeare and Jonson among writers in the seventeenth century.

CLASS 19

Criticism of the works of Shakespeare or Jonson. Passages of this type are not simply passing condemnation or praise of the man's work in general, but a notation of particulars of excellence or inferiority. The most familiar allusions in this class are the numerous passages in Dryden's essays and prefaces, but most of them are too long for quotation.

The Friends too of our great Dramatick Writer, *Shakespear*, will not be perswaded, but that even his Monstrous Irregularities were Conducive to those Shining Beauties, which abound in most of his Plays; and that if he had been more a Critick, he had been less a Poet.[33]—T. R., *An Essay, concerning Critical and Curious Learning* (1698), pp. 30–31.

Our Poets, continued he, represent the Modern little Actions of Debauchees, as *Ben Johnson* presented the Humours of his Tankard Bearer, his Pauls Walkers, and his Collegiate Ladies, &c. things then known and familiar to every Bodies Notice; and so are these now, and consequently delightful to the times, as Pictures of Faces well known and remarkable. These, Answered *Julio*, were *Ben Johnsons* Weaknesses, and have been as such sufficiently exploded by our New fashion'd Wits, and therefore methinks they should not be imitated by them of all Men Living. Such Representations are like a Painters taking a Picture after the Life in the Apparel then Worn, which becomes Ungraceful or Ridiculous in the next Age, when the Fashion is out.—[JAMES WRIGHT], *Country Conversations* (1694), pp. 9–10.[34]

DISTRIBUTION OF ALLUSIONS
IN CLASS 19

	Shake-speare	Jonson
1601–1610	0	2
1611–1620	1	0
1621–1630	0	0
1631–1640	0	3
1641–1650	2	0
1651–1660	1	0
1661–1670	5	10
1671–1680	11	9
1681–1690	2	7
1691–1700	14	7
Undated	0	0
Totals	36	38

The Jonson majority in allusions of this type is smaller than might have been expected in the light of the figures for Classes 1 and 2, yet an examination of the distribution by decades gives a fairly clear indication of the reason for the difference. In the two former classes— the praise of Jonson and the poems and prose passages addressed to him—the allusions are very numerous in

[33] This passage is also classified as Class 1.

[34] Other examples will be found in Vol. II, pp. 62–63 and 235–36.

the first six decades of the century, outnumbering those to Shakespeare 5 to 1 and 4 to 1, respectively. Though in the decades after the Restoration there are also more allusions to Jonson than to Shakespeare in those two classes, the majority is much smaller, about 7 to 4 and 7 to 6. Now allusions of Class 19 are not characteristic of the first half of the century at all; writers of this peri od clearly preferred Jonson to Shakespeare, as the figures in Classes 1 and 2 demonstrate, but they rarely gave specific reasons for their preference. Not until after the Restoration did critics of English *drama* become sufficiently articulate to write the extended dramatic criticism in which allusions of this type are usually found. By that time Jonson's reputation, though still dominant, was not overwhelmingly greater than Shakespeare's.

A second important factor in the situation is John Dryden. His championing of Shakespeare in his essays and prefaces was probably the most important single influence in the burgeoning of Shakespeare's reputation after the Restoration; in allusions of this class his significance is very clear. In the two decades of the sixties and seventies, three-fourths of the allusions of this class to Shakespeare come from the pen of John Dryden, only about one-fourth of those to Jonson. Indeed, one might hazard the guess that Dryden was not only largely responsible for the rapid growth of Shakespeare's reputation after 1668 but that much of the modern misconception of the comparative reputations of Shakespeare and Jonson in Dryden's lifetime is also due to the author of *An Essay of Dramatick Poesie*. Dryden's critical writings are much more widely known now than those of any of his contemporaries; his remarks on Shakespeare and Jonson are remembered when those of Shadwell and Howard and Oldham are forgotten. It is not easy to remember that, though Dryden's dramatic criticism is the best of the period, it is not therefore the most characteristic.

CLASS 20

Criticism of a single work of Shakespeare or Jonson. This classification differs from the preceding in that only one work is discussed instead of the qualities or shortcomings of the dramatist's work as a whole. Dryden's "Examen of the *Silent Woman*" in his *Essay of Dramatick Poesie* is the most familiar example. Most of the passages of this type, like Dryden's "Examen," are too long to quote. Probably the shortest of all is one which barely qualifies—Jonson's comment on *The Winter's Tale* in 1618.

Sheakspear jn a play brought jn a number of men saying they had suffered Shipwrack jn Bohemia, wher y^r is no Sea neer by some 100 Miles.— "Ben Jonson's Conversations with William Drummond of Hawthornden," in HERFORD and SIMPSON, *Ben Jonson*, I, 138.[35]

Allusions of this class might have been expected to approximate in number and distribution those of the former. The difference in distribution is not very puzzling; the most abnormal aspect is the 8 allusions to Jonson in the first decade. These 8 allusions account not only for the unusual proportion before 1660 but also for most of the increased majority of Jonson allusions in the class as compared with Class 19. Six of the 8 allusions come from the commendatory poems written for the first edition of *Sejanus*. The criticism of the play they set forth is due not to an unusual development of critical

[35] Other examples will be found in Vol. II, pp. 222–23 and 240–42.

interest in the first decade but to the reception of the play in the theater. Jonson's friends, George Chapman, Hugh Holland, William Strachey, and three other anonymous contributors, felt called upon to defend his tragedy against the hostile public which, as they point out, had hissed it in the theater; and their defense in-

DISTRIBUTION OF ALLUSIONS IN CLASS 20

	Shakespeare	Jonson
1601–1610	0	8
1611–1620	1	1
1621–1630	1	0
1631–1640	2	1
1641–1650	1	0
1651–1660	0	0
1661–1670	0	6
1671–1680	3	6
1681–1690	3	2
1691–1700	7	7
Undated	1	0
Totals	19	31

cludes comment upon particular virtues of the play— or allusions of Class 20. Without these 6 allusions, the number before 1650 is almost exactly the same as the number in Class 19, and the ratio of Shakespeare to Jonson allusions does not differ greatly.

Our consideration of the variety of classes into which allusions to Shakespeare and to Jonson fall in the seventeenth century has high-lighted several aspects of their reputations. Perhaps least significant is the fact that in fifteen classes there are more references to Jonson than to Shakespeare; in six, more to Shakespeare than to Jonson; and in one an equal number to each. More significant is the particular kind of allusion in which each poet's majority occurs and the extent of the majority.

In seven classes of allusions, Jonson's majority is overwhelming, i.e., more than five times as many in groups under 50, more than twice as many in the groups of 50–300, and a majority of more than 100 in the groups containing from 300 to 1,300 allusions. These types in which Jonson overwhelmingly dominates are allusions offering the highest praise, poems or long prose passages devoted wholly to him, commonplace books and anthologies quoting his works, references to his plays by name, business records of his performances, letters to him, and records of honors proposed or bestowed. The extent of the Jonson majorities in these classes suggests strongly the following general opinions among seventeenth-century writers: Jonson had no serious rival as the greatest English dramatist; Jonson's compositions were more suitable than Shakespeare's for the commonplace book of a gentleman; Jonson's individual plays were more widely known and admired than Shakespeare's; Jonson's pieces were far more suitable for presentation before a courtly audience than Shakespeare's; Jonson was not only much more widely honored in his lifetime than Shakespeare, but mementos of him were cherished, while those of Shakespeare were not.

In two classes of allusions the references are overwhelmingly greater to Shakespeare than to Jonson, namely, allusions to apocryphal plays and to individual characters. As we have noted, the first of these is not very significant, indicating only that there are about ten times as many plays in the Shakespearean apocrypha as in the Jonsonian—a fact sufficiently clear without recourse to allusions. The allusions in the second class are highly significant, however, especially when considered in conjunction with the number of references to Jonson as the greatest dramatist and to his individual plays. Though Jonson had the higher general reputation and though his plays were more widely known, Shakespeare's characters still made a much deeper impression than those of Jonson. Under the circumstances this wealth of allusion to Shakespeare's characters is much more impressive than a similar preference for Jonson's characters would have been, for writers are paying homage to Shakespeare's unequaled powers of characterization in spite of themselves. In this class of allusion only does Shakespeare's seventeenth-century general reputation approach his modern one.

In six classes of allusions Jonson has a clear majority, i.e., 70–80 per cent in groups under 50, 55–70 per cent in groups of 50–300. These classes are allusions naming Jonson or Shakespeare and two or three others not of the triumvirate as a standard of greatness; lists of literary men in which none is particularly distinguished from the others; literary or social references to performances of his plays or masques; criticism of individual plays; biographical records and anecdotes; and miscellaneous allusions. These majorities suggest, though not quite so emphatically as the others, that writers making lists of English poets generally thought of Jonson before Shakespeare; that performances of Jonson's plays and masques were more popular social topics than performances of Shakespeare's; that individual merits of Jonson's plays seemed a more deserving subject than the individual merits of Shakespeare's; that Jonson as a man was more widely cherished in records and anecdotes than Shakespeare; and that Jonson's name came more easily to mind for casual reference than Shakespeare's.

There are three classes in which the clear majority of the allusions is to Shakespeare: quotations for purposes of illustration; plagiarism from his works or burlesques of his lines; and references to his characters as acting roles. The first class is the most significant, because there are over 200 allusions in it, while the other two are so small that the discovery of 25 or 30 new allusions could change the situation completely. These majorities suggest that, in spite of Jonson's great reputation and the hundreds of copies of his works in anthologies and commonplace books, Shakespeare's single lines were recognized as more quotable than Jonson's. The same suggestion is made, though less clearly because of the small numbers involved, by the Shakespearean majority in the second class. The third class reiterates, somewhat faintly, the popularity of Shakespeare's characters already observed.

Finally, in four classes of allusions the numbers are so nearly equal that no clear preference is shown. These classes are allusions to Shakespeare and Jonson as members of the triumvirate, in which Shakespeare leads by 3; lists of literary men in which Shakespeare or Jonson is given especial distinction, in which Jonson leads by 5; biographical accounts, in which the numbers are even; and criticism of the dramatist's works in general, where Jonson leads by 2. In the last three classes the numbers are so small that the discovery of a dozen new allusions could completely change the proportions.

CHAPTER VI
THE COMPARATIVE POPULARITY OF
INDIVIDUAL PLAYS

THE PRECEDING CHAPTERS HAVE MADE IT REASONABLY
clear that to writers of the seventeenth century Jonson
was better known and more highly respected than
Shakespeare. Not until the final decade were Shakespeare
and his creations mentioned so often as Jonson and
his, and even then they were not so frequently praised.
Not only was Jonson mentioned oftener, quoted oftener,[1] and praised oftener, but his individual plays and
poems were named more frequently than Shakespeare's,
though his canon is smaller. Only in the references to
his characters does Shakespeare have anything like the
unquestioned acclaim which seems to us now so inevitably his.

A little study of the allusions to individual works and
characters of the two great dramatists will throw still
further light on their reputations in the seventeenth
century. Did Shakespeare make a greater impression in
the time with his comedies or with his tragedies? Was
Jonson's reputation based entirely on his great comedies? Which particular plays were most frequently men-

---

[1] That is, Jonson's combined total in Classes 6, 7, and 8 is greater than Shakespeare's. Since, as we have noticed, Jonson is quoted in commonplace books and
other manuscript sources many times as often as Shakespeare, and since such sources
are the most inadequately explored of all allusion fields, we can be reasonably confident that in the future more new quotations from Jonson than from Shakespeare
will be turned up.

tioned? Which characters? The answers to such questions as these are at least suggested by the accompanying summaries of allusions.

The first list shows the individual works of Shakespeare and Jonson ranked in the order of popularity in the seventeenth century as indicated by extant allusions. Plays and poems referred to less than 8 times have not been included in this list.[2]

The evidence of these collected allusions to individual works of Shakespeare and Jonson affords clear-cut proof that Jonson's plays were much the better known in the seventeenth century. Six of Jonson's plays, besides the masques and the poems, were more commonly referred to than anything of Shakespeare's; Jonson's best-known play was mentioned more than twice as often as Shakespeare's. Even this comparison is an understatement, for Jonson's most popular play was unadulterated Jonson, while a number of the allusions to *The Tempest* are to either the Dryden and Davenant version or the operatic version, and the most specific comments sometimes refer to elements in the play for which Shake-

---

[2] The plays and poems to which there are 7 allusions or less are, in order of popularity: *The Arraignment of Paris; Cromwell; Cymbeline; The Fall of Mortimer; King John,* Parts 1 and 2; *Coriolanus; The Merchant of Venice; The Birth of Merlin; Locrine; The Merry Devil of Edmonton; Mucedorus; The Puritan Widow; All's Well That Ends Well; Antony and Cleopatra; As You Like It; Grammar; Two Gentlemen of Verona; The Two Noble Kinsmen; The Case Is Altered; King John; Poems* (Shakespeare); *The Puritan; Richard Crookback; The Spanish Tragedy* Additions; *The Beggars' Bush* (attributed to Jonson); *The Chances* (attributed to Shakespeare); *Edward II; Edward III; Edward IV; Hieronimo* (attributed to Shakespeare); *Hoffman* (attributed to Shakespeare); *The Isle of Dogs; The Passionate Pilgrim; Thierry and Theodoret* (attributed to Jonson); *The Roman Actor* (attributed to Shakespeare); *A Trick To Catch the Old One* (attributed to Shakespeare).

When the number of allusions represented gets as small as for these plays, the order does not mean much; the discovery of a very few new allusions could change it completely.

ALLUSIONS TO INDIVIDUAL WORKS OF
SHAKESPEARE AND JONSON[3]

Masques[4].	112	Taming of the Shrew.	15
Catiline.	89	Much Ado about Nothing[9].	14
Volpone.	73	Richard II.	14
Alchemist.	67	Winter's Tale.	14
Silent Woman.	62	Julius Caesar.	13
Sejanus.	59	Rape of Lucrece.	12
Poems (Jonson)[3].	52	Measure for Measure.	12
Bartholomew Fair.	48	Richard III.	12
Tempest[6].	40	King Lear.	11
Othello.	37	Love's Labour's Lost.	11
Macbeth[6].	34	Sad Shepherd.	11
Henry IV, 1 and 2[7].	30	Tale of a Tub.	11
Poetaster.	28	Timon of Athens.	11
Every Man in His Humour.	25	Troilus and Cressida[6].	11
Hamlet.	25	Cynthia's Revels.	10
Henry VI,[6] 1, 2, and 3[7].	24	Eastward Ho!.	10
Pericles.	24	Widow.	10
Venus and Adonis.	24	Discoveries.	9
Henry VIII.	23	Henry V.	9
New Inn.	23	Horace.	9
Magnetic Lady.	22	London Prodigal.	9
Merry Wives of Windsor.	22	Sir John Oldcastle.	9
Comedy of Errors[8].	18	Twelfth Night.	9
Devil Is an Ass.	18	Yorkshire Tragedy.	9
Midsummer-Night's Dream.	18	Staple of News.	8
Every Man Out of His Humour	15	Titus Andronicus.	8
Romeo and Juliet.	15		

[3] These allusion figures at once invite comparison with those given in *The Shakspere Allusion-Book*, II, 540. The first sixteen there are:

Hamlet.	95	Richard III.	36
Henry IV, 1 and 2.	69	Richard II.	35
Venus and Adonis.	61	Midsummer-Night's Dream.	35
Romeo and Juliet.	61	Julius Caesar.	35
Othello.	56	Henry VI, 1, 2, and 3.	32
Lucrece.	41	Much Ado about Nothing.	30
Tempest.	40	Henry VIII.	29
Macbeth.	37	Pericles.	28

Part of the difference between my figures and those in *The Shakspere Allusion-Book* is accounted for by the fact that Munro included sixteenth-century allusions, as I have not, and part by the hundreds of allusions brought forward since his collection; but most important is his counting of many allusions which have been re-

[Footnotes continued on following page]

speare was not responsible.[10] Though many of the allusions to *The Tempest* do not themselves contain statements showing definitely which version the writer had
in mind, it is pretty clear that the revisions and not

---

jected here as parallel passages, proverbial expressions, publication data, or vague
and uncertain statements. Most eloquent is the difference between his *Hamlet* figures and mine. Since *Hamlet* has long been our most familiar play, imaginary parallels to its lines and situations are most commonly reported.

[4] In a list like this it is awkward to have all Jonson's masques lumped together,
but it is the most accurate reflection of the way in which men of the seventeenth
century seem to have thought of them. Allusions generally do not distinguish them
but say "as in Jonson's masques" or "the gipsy in Jonson's masque." Separate list-
ings would eliminate a large number of the allusions and tend to conceal the place
they had in references of the time.

[5] Like the masques, the poems are generally not particularized in allusions.

[6] In many instances it is impossible to tell whether Shakespeare's original or the
Restoration recension is referred to; even when the revision is clearly intended, the
allusion has been counted for Shakespeare's play.

[7] Since, in the majority of instances, it is impossible to tell which part is referred
to, the fairest procedure is to count all together.

[8] I feel confident that this group of words was often used without thought of
Shakespeare's play, just as it is today; but so long as I cannot prove that the expression is proverbial it seems fairest to accept all the allusions.

[9] "Much ado about nothing" seems to be used as a proverbial expression, just as
"a comedy of errors" is, but I cannot prove that it antedates Shakespeare's play.

[10] A writer in the *Athenian Mercury* considers the question:
"*Suppose a Man and Woman were shut up in a room together, who had never seen
nor heard of the difference of Sexes before, how d'ye think they'd behave themselves?—
wou'd they—*

"Answ.: We say . . . . that we *don't know what to say.* We are very unwilling to
send the Ladies to *Daphnis* and *Chloe* for Information—that Book is too *waggish* in
some places, and not *spiritual* enough for 'em: As for the *Tempest*, that don't come
up to the Question, tho *Mirande* and *Hypolito* are pretty fair for't, who had never
seen, tho' they had heard of *Man* and *Woman*" (*Athenian Mercury*, IV, No. 13
[Tuesday, November 10, 1691], 2, reported by John Munro, "More Shakspere
Allusions," *Modern Philology*, XIII [January, 1916], 168).
In Durfey's *The Marriage-Hater Match'd* (1692), Darewell says (p. 50):
"I told ye she was a High Flyer too, that is, I have seen her upon a Machine in
the *Tempest.*
"L. Brain: In the *Tempest*, why then I suppose I may seek her Fortune in the
Inchanted Island."

Shakespeare's original are generally intended. The best evidence for this conclusion lies in the fact that 90 per cent of the seventeenth-century allusions to *The Tempest* occur in the period 1667–1700, i.e., after the first production of the Davenant-Dryden version;[11] and most of the allusions in the first two years of this period come from the pen of Samuel Pepys, who clearly alluded to the current stage version.

That *Catiline* was most familiar of all the plays of the two dramatists in the seventeenth century ought to surprise no student of the period. There are allusions to it in every decade of the century after its composition in 1611. Cotgrave quoted it nearly twice as often as any play of Shakespeare's.[12] Robert Hills wrote in his commendatory verses for Robert Baron's *Mirza* in 1647 (sig. A₄),

> Mean time, who'l number our best *Playes* aright
> First *CATALINE*, then let him *MIRZA* write,
> So mix your names: in the third place must be
> *SEIANUS*, or *the next* that comes from *thee*.

Baron himself says:

> . . . . not without the example of the matchless *Johnson*, who, in his *Catiline* (which miraculous *Poem* I propose as my pattern) makes *Sylla*'s Ghost perswade *Catiline* to do what *Hannibal* could not wish.—*Mirza* (1647), sig. M₁.

Edward Howard held a similar opinion in 1671:

> I do not find but the highest of our English Tragedies (as *Cataline*, *The Maids Tragedy*, *Rollo*, *The Cardinal and Traytor*) considerable enough to

---

[11] Arthur H. Nethercot, *Sir William D'avenant, Poet Laureate and Playwright-Manager* (1938), p. 399.

[12] Thirty-three times (see my "John Cotgrave's *English Treasury of Wit and Language* and the Elizabethan Drama," *Studies in Philology*, XL [April, 1943], 202). Such quotations without acknowledgment of source are not, of course, counted as allusions to the play, but to the dramatist only.

be rank'd with the best of these.—Preface, *The Womens Conquest* (1671), sig. A₃ᵛ.

There can be little doubt that not *Hamlet*, *Lear*, *Othello*, or *Macbeth*, but *Catiline* was the premier English tragedy in the minds of seventeenth-century writers.

Volpone's distinguished position as the ranking comedy, though it accords better with modern opinion than *Catiline*'s, is not quite so unchallenged. Pepys, indeed, had called it "a most excellent play, the best I think I ever saw," but Pepys was not niggardly with his superlatives; and other writers, though mentioning *Volpone* more frequently than other comedies, do not praise it so often as they do *Catiline*, *Sejanus*, *The Alchemist*, and *The Silent Woman*.

The Alchemist, in particular, receives more specific praise in the century than *Volpone* does. Shirley wrote a prologue for it when he was working for the Werburgh Street Theatre in Dublin, beginning

> The Alchemist, a play for strength of wit,
> And true art, made to shame what hath been writ
> In former ages; I except no worth
> Of what or Greek or Latins have brought forth;
> Is now to be presented to your ear,
> For which I wish each man were a Muse here,
> To know, and in his soul be fit to be
> Judge of this masterpiece of comedy.
>
> —*Poems* (1646), ed. GIFFORD, VI, 490–91

James Howell, in writing to Jonson of the poet's divine fury, says: "You were mad when you writ your *Fox*, and madder when you writ your *Alchymist*."[13] Robert Herrick in his epigram on Jonson speaks of the ignorance that came to the theater after Jonson's death:

---

[13] *Epistolae Ho-Elianae*, ed. Joseph Jacobs (1890), p. 267. The letter is dated June 27, 1629.

> and that monstrous sin
> Of deep and arrant ignorance came in:
> Such ignorance as theirs was who once hist
> At thy unequall'd play, the Alchemist:
> —*Hesperides* (1648), ed. ALFRED POLLARD (1891), p. 188

Edward Howard in a discussion of the methods of "learned *Johnson*" calls the play "that great work of his the Alchymist."[14] Robert Gale Noyes says: "Of all the comedies of Jonson *The Alchemist* had the most brilliant stage-history . . . . it was acted oftener than any other Jonsonian play."[15] Noyes is speaking of the entire period 1660–1776, but the popularity of *The Alchemist* was well developed before the beginning of the eighteenth century.

The reputation of *The Silent Woman* is sufficiently familiar from Dryden's *Examen* and the various comments of Pepys.[16] Both this play and *Bartholomew Fair* have a much higher proportion of their allusions after the Restoration than do the preceding three. In both cases the subject matter must have had a particular appeal for audiences under Charles II, Samuel Pepys in the case of *Bartholomew Fair* to the contrary notwithstanding.

The popularity of *The Tempest*, as already noted, is a somewhat dubious measure of Shakespeare's appeal. The *Othello* allusions are based on much more solidly Shakespearean material and are more evenly distributed through the century. Indeed, in the allusions up through

---

[14] *The Womens Conquest* (1671), Preface, sigs. b₂ᵛ–b₃.

[15] *Ben Jonson on the English Stage, 1660–1776* (1935), p. 103.

[16] See above, pp. 52–53.

1680, *Othello* is Shakespeare's most popular play.[17]
Samuel Sheppard ranked it with *Catiline* in 1651 in his
verses on Davenant's *Albovine:*

> *Shakespeares Othello, Johnsons Cataline,*
> Would lose their luster, were thy *Albovine*
> Placed betwixt them.
> —*Epigrams Theological, Philosophical, and*
> *Romantick* (1651), Book 4, Epigram 30

Thomas Rymer suggests its position in his *Tragedies of
the Last Age Considered* (1678):

I provided me some of those *Master pieces* of Wit, so renown'd every-
where, and so edifying to the *Stage:* I mean the choicest and most applaud-
ed *English Tragedies* of this last age; as *Rollo; A King and no King;* the
Maids Tragedy by *Beaumont* and *Fletcher: Othello,* and *Julius Cæsar,* by
Shakespear; and *Cataline* by Worthy *Ben* [2d ed. (1692), pp. 1–2].

Though Rymer grew weary of the slaughter before he
came to his analysis of *Othello* in *The Tragedies of the
Last Age Considered,* he got around to it several years
later in *A Short View of Tragedy.*[18] His opening state-

[17] The number of allusions to the most popular plays in the first eight decades of
the century may have some general interest. They are as follows:

Catiline	67	Poetaster	14
Sejanus	47	Henry IV, 1 and 2	13
Volpone	47	Magnetic Lady	13
Alchemist	45	Merry Wives of Windsor	13
Silent Woman	41	Poems (Jonson)	13
Masques	31	Comedy of Errors	12
Bartholomew Fair	27	Every Man in His Humour	12
Othello	21	New Inn	12
Macbeth	20	Hamlet	11
Venus and Adonis	20	Every Man Out of His	
Tempest	17	Humour	8
Henry VIII	16	Romeo and Juliet	8
Pericles	15		

Except for the increase in popularity of *The Tempest* and the decline of *Venus and
Adonis,* the relative positions of the various plays is more like that for the century as
a whole than might have been expected. Particularly notable is the fact that in each
list the same six plays of Jonson outrank Shakespeare's most popular piece.

[18] (1693 [for 1692]), pp. 86–146. This long discussion of *Othello* with its reiteration
of the names of the characters gives Desdemona, Othello, Iago, Cassio, Roderigo,

ment (p. 86) again points to the popularity of the play: "From all the Tragedies acted on our English Stage, *Othello* is said to bear the Bell away." To Rymer, of course, this popularity is entirely undeserved; and he sneers his way through the play in the all too familiar fashion of the critic who relies on his dogma because he cannot trust his perceptions. In spite of his contempt, however, Rymer has testified to the popularity of *Othello* with sufficient positiveness to confirm the implications of the allusion count.

Macbeth and *Henry IV, Parts 1 and 2*, are both like *The Tempest* in that their position is not due solely to appreciation of Shakespeare's original play. The *Macbeth* allusions are mostly, it would appear, to Davenant's operatic version;[19] for less than 10 per cent of them occur before 1663, the presumed date of Davenant's revision. An examination of Pepys's comments on the play, which he saw nine times, suggests that his admiration was generally elicited by the contemporary additions rather than by Shakespeare's original. In the case of *Henry IV* the allusions are generally incidental to references to Falstaff, the most popular character of the century; it is seldom mentioned for itself alone. The fact that there are more than four times as many allusions to the fat knight as to the play is a further suggestion that *Henry IV* appeared to the seventeenth century as the tail to Falstaff's kite.

Ludovico, and Brabantio positions misleadingly high in the ranks of Shakespearean and Jonsonian characters. Rymer's discussion does not, however, unduly affect the position of the piece in the play-allusions list, for his long analysis is counted as only one allusion to *Othello*.

[19] See Nethercot, *op. cit.*, pp. 391–95.

The familiarity of *Poetaster* is largely a result of the War of the Theaters and of the appreciation of Jonson's jibe in introducing the play with an armed prologue. Few allusions express any great admiration for the play itself.

Every Man in His Humour was really more widely appreciated and more frequently acted than *Poetaster*. Pepys's comment on *Every Man in His Humour*—"wherein is the greatest propriety of speech that ever I read in my life" (February 9, 1666/67)—is not uncharacteristic.

The position of *Hamlet*, fifteenth in the list, however incredible it may seem in the twentieth century, is not unsupported by other evidence. When John Cotgrave collected quotations from contemporary drama for his *English Treasury of Wit and Language* (1655), he selected more passages from fourteen other plays than from Hamlet.[20] And though those fourteen plays, except for *Catiline* and *Sejanus*, were not the same as the fourteen which outrank *Hamlet* here, they are all by dramatists whom we now consider inferior to Shakespeare—Greville, Webster, Jonson, Chapman, Dekker, Tourneur, Daniel, Suckling, and Marston.

The positions of both the *Henry VI* plays and *Pericles* are probably higher than seventeenth-century opinion of Shakespeare's works would really warrant. The rank of *Henry VI* above its betters is due to the fact that the allusions to three different plays are all of necessity lumped together here, and to the further fact that certain of the allusions may well refer to John Crowne's Henry VI plays. Though *Pericles* undoubtedly ranked

---

[20] See *Studies in Philology*, XL (April, 1943), 202.

higher in the seventeenth century than it does now, I think its position here is probably due to the intrusion, in spite of my efforts, of certain allusions which really refer to fictional or historic accounts of Pericles.

Venus and Adonis falls lower in the list than one with a knowledge of the poem's early popularity and the editions it went through would expect. If all allusions to Shakespeare before 1701 had been included, *Venus and Adonis* would undoubtedly rank higher. These figures —which exclude all allusions before 1601—show that the poem's vogue was largely a sixteenth-century one. Though I have not counted the number of quotations from the various plays and poems, I have noted in checking them that there are more quotations from *Venus and Adonis* than from several of the works which rank above it in the list.

The rest of the works on the list are not sufficiently prominent to warrant individual discussion, but a few of them merit a remark or two.

Henry VIII owes its rank chiefly to Restoration performances; all but 2 or 3 of the allusions before the Restoration occur because it happened to be the play in performance when the first Globe burned.

The place of *The Magnetic Lady* and *The New Inn* again gives pause to the modern reader. Even Jonson's "dotages" are referred to more often than *King Lear*, *Antony and Cleopatra*, *As You Like It*, *Twelfth Night*, and *The Merchant of Venice*.

Romeo and Juliet, like *Venus and Adonis*, would have ranked much higher had sixteenth-century allusions been included, and so would *Richard II* and *Richard III*.

Finally, the low estimation of Shakespeare's comedies

is too conspicuous to ignore. Only one of them—*The Tempest*—ranks any higher than twentieth, and that play, as we have seen, appears to owe its position more to Dryden and Davenant than to Shakespeare. Some of the comedies most popular in modern times—*As You Like It*, *The Merchant of Venice*, and *Twelfth Night*— seem scarcely known at all in the seventeenth century. The reason is certainly not any contempt for comedy. The high rank of *Volpone*, *The Alchemist*, *The Silent Woman*, and *Bartholomew Fair* and the great achievement of Restoration comedy are clear proof of general interest in the form. It is Shakespearean comedy, or perhaps more accurately Shakespearean romantic comedy, which is ignored.

CHAPTER VII

THE COMPARATIVE POPULARITY OF IN-DIVIDUAL CHARACTERS

THE ALLUSIONS TO THE CHARACTERS OF SHAKESPEARE and Jonson present a very different reputation-picture from that of the plays and poems, as has already been demonstrated by the summaries of allusions in Classes 10, 11, and 11*a*.[1] The numbers of allusions to individual characters throw further light on particular differences between the reputations of Shakespeare and of Jonson in the seventeenth century. The list on page 120 shows the characters ranked in order of the number of allusions to each. Characters mentioned less than 5 times have not been included in the list.[2]

Falstaff was clearly most famous of all the characters of Shakespeare and Jonson in the seventeenth century. This fact ought to surprise no reader familiar with the literature of the time, but the overwhelming dominance of his position has perhaps not been so obvious. It might have been guessed from Rowe's statement in 1709—"*Falstaff* is allow'd by every body to be a Master-

---

[1] See above, pp. 81–87.

[2] The characters named 3 or 4 times are, in order of popularity: Asper, Boling-broke–Henry IV, Bottom, Mosca, Adam Overdo, Portia (*Caesar*), Tucca, Ursula, Wolsey, Beatrice, Bobadil, Buckingham (*Henry VIII*), Carlo Buffone, Christopher Sly, Cicero (*Catiline*), Crites, Dauphine, Doll Tearsheet, Epicoene, Hector, Hugh Evans, Littlewit, Lodovico, Miranda, Mrs. Ford, Mrs. Otter, Mrs. Page, Pug, Richard II, Romeo, Shallow, Tribulation Wholesome, Ann Page, and Apemantus. The characters named only once or twice do not seem worth recording.

ALLUSIONS TO CHARACTERS

Falstaff[3]	131	Witches (*Macbeth*)	9
Othello	55	Antony[5]	8
Desdemona	45	Bartholomew Cokes	8
Brutus	44	Hotspur	8
Iago	42	Sir John Daw	8
Cassio	29	Catiline	7
Hamlet	27	Collegiate Ladies	7
Doll Common	21	Otter	7
Julius Caesar	19	Bardolph[6]	6
Morose	18	Cethegus	6
Trinculo	17	Ghost (*Hamlet*)	6
Sir Politic Would-Be	16	Pistol[7]	6
Prince Hal[4]	15	Polonius	6
Cassius	14	Quickly-Hostess[8]	6
Face	13	Richard III	6
Caliban	11	Sycorax	6
Macbeth	10	Ananias	5
Sir Amorous La-Foole	10	Cob	5
Subtle	10	Crispinus	5
Sylla's Ghost	10	Dauphine	5
Volpone	10	Doge of Venice	5
Brabantio	9	Henry VIII	5
Ophelia	9	John of Wrotham[9]	5
Rabbi Zeal-of-the-Land Busy	9	Juliet	5
Roderigo	9	Stephano	5
Truewit	9		

[3] In many allusions it is impossible to tell whether the character in *Henry IV, Part 1*, *Henry IV, Part 2*, or *The Merry Wives of Windsor* is intended. Even when the particular play is indicated, however, all allusions have been counted together.

[4] Since most allusions do not name the play, all allusions to Prince Hal or Henry V from any of the plays containing the character have been counted together.

[5] Allusions to Antony in *Julius Caesar* and *Antony and Cleopatra* have been counted together.

[6] Allusions to Bardolph have all been counted together, whether they refer to the character in *Henry IV, Part 1*, *Henry IV, Part 2*, *Henry V*, or *The Merry Wives of Windsor*.

[7] Allusions to Pistol in *Henry IV, Part 2*, *Henry V*, and *The Merry Wives of Windsor* have been counted together.

[8] Allusions to the Hostess or Mistress Quickly in *Henry IV, Part 1*, *Henry IV, Part 2*, *Henry V*, and *The Merry Wives of Windsor* have been counted together.

[9] Sir John is the only character in the list from an apocryphal play, *Sir John Oldcastle*.

piece";[10] but Rowe was something of a special pleader, and his remarks about other Shakespearean characters are not borne out by seventeenth-century allusions. The typical allusions to Falstaff, furthermore, are not the self-conscious praise of the type usually bestowed upon *Catiline.* They are, for the most part, passing references obviously intended to enlighten the reader by a comparison or to amuse him by reminding him of the escapades or characteristics of Shakespeare's fat knight.

> Our Keepers knew no hurt, unlesse 't had bin
> Drinking of Sack, honest *Iack Falstaffes* sinne.[11]

> D'ye run away, b' *instinct* like Sir *John Falstaffe*,
> And *stare*, and *huffe*, and *puff*, as if y' had been
> Mauld, by th' *unluckie Rogues* in *Kendall Green.*[12]

> My brave comradoes, Knights of [the] tatter'd Fleece,
> Like Falstafs Regiment, you have one shirt among you.[13]

"Well," says he, "if this will not do, I will say, as Sir J. Falstaffe did to the Prince, 'Tell your father, that if he do not like this let him kill the next Piercy himself.' "[14]

I cannot but observe, Mr. *Bayes*, this admirable way (like fat *Sir John Falstaffe*'s singular dexterity in sinking) that you have of answering whole Books and Discources, how pithy and knotty soever, in a line or two, nay sometimes with a word.[15]

[10] Nicholas Rowe, *The Works of Mr. William Shakespear in Six Volumes* (1709), I, xvii.

[11] *The Cambridge Royallist Imprisoned*, July 31, 1643, sig. A₄ (cited by Hyder E. Rollins, "Shakespeare Allusions," *Notes and Queries: Twelfth Series*, X [1922], 224).

[12] "On Oxford Visitors, 1648," in Henry Bold, *Poems* (1664), p. 164 (cited by John Munro, "More Shakspere Allusions," *Modern Philology*, XIII [January, 1916], 150).

[13] Thomas Randolph, *Hey for Honesty, Down with Knavery* (1651), Act III, scene 1, p. 22.

[14] Samuel Pepys, *Diary*, August 29, 1666.

[15] Andrew Marvel, *The Rehearsal Transprosd* (1672), p. 190.

Fat *Falstaffe* was never set harder by the Prince for a *Reason*, when he answer'd, that *if* Reasons *grew as thick as* Blackberries, *he wou'd not give one.*[16]

I can answer for no body's palat but my own: and cannot help saying with the fat Knight in Henry the Fourth If sack and sugar is a sin, the Lord have mercy on the wicked.[17]

Such characteristic allusions as these reveal an affectionate familiarity with Falstaff which is not generally found in the allusions to other characters. There is no hint that the author feels he is displaying the impeccability of his own literary taste or the soundness of his training in the classics—suggestions which are frequently to be found in the Jonson allusions. Even before the Civil War Falstaff had become a part of the literary heritage of the language, and his words and deeds could be expected to have a wide enough familiarity to assist any author who chose to call upon him.

The five characters next in the list after Falstaff were all less familiar in the century than the figures would indicate. In each case a large number of the allusions come from a single long discussion in which the character is mentioned again and again. Othello, Desdemona, Iago, and Cassio, as well as Brabantio (twenty-second), Roderigo (twenty-fifth), and the Doge of Venice (forty-seventh) owe their positions to Thomas Rymer's analysis of *Othello* in his *A Short View of Tragedy*.[18] Rymer praises neither the characters nor the play in this discussion but vigorously ridicules both. Similarly, in

---

[16] John Dryden, *The Vindication of the Duke of Guise* (1683), p. 48 (cited by Munro, *op. cit.*, p. 163).

[17] Anonymous, *A Collection of Miscellany Poems, Letters, etc.* (1699), p. 327, letter dated "June 2 92" (cited by G. Thorn-Drury, *Some Seventeenth Century Allusions to Shakespeare and His Works Not Hitherto Collected* [1920], p. 46).

[18] (1693 [for 1692]), pp. 86–146.

the following chapter Rymer ridicules *Julius Caesar*,[19] though not at such length, with frequent allusions to characters and situations in *Othello*. Though all the references to plays and characters of Shakespeare and Jonson in these two chapters are bona fide allusions, the normal counting of them tends to give undue weight to Rymer in the consideration of Shakespeare's characters. In the play figures, Rymer's discussions count as only one allusion to each play, which gives a fairer estimate. No Jonson character is mentioned more than once in the discussion of *Catiline*, but the enthusiasm with which Rymer belabors *Othello* and *Julius Caesar* leads him to bring in the characters again and again.

A somewhat more accurate picture of the familiarity of these characters in the seventeenth century might be presented, therefore, if Rymer's *A Short View of Tragedy* were not considered and all the allusions there to characters of Shakespeare and Jonson subtracted from the above totals. Such a modification gives the standings shown in the list on page 124.

The most notable change in the altered figures is the enhanced prominence of Falstaff, who now has nearly four times as many allusions as the next character. Moreover, second place instead of fourth is taken by Brutus, and third instead of seventh by Hamlet. Probably no modern critic would hold Brutus in such high regard; but the fact that he is the leading character in Shakespeare's most familiar Roman play was more significant in the seventeenth century than it is now. Perhaps the fact that Brutus bears some likeness to the protagonists of heroic tragedy was also of significance,

19 Chap. viii, pp. 147-59.

for the largest proportion of the Brutus allusions comes from the last two decades of the century. Indeed, a larger proportion of the Brutus allusions comes from these last two decades than of the allusions for any

CHARACTER ALLUSIONS EXCLUSIVE OF RYMER'S
SHORT VIEW

Falstaff	131	Witches (*Macbeth*)	9
Brutus	34	Bartholomew Cokes	8
Hamlet	27	Hotspur	8
Doll Common	21	Sir John Daw	8
Julius Caesar	19	Collegiate Ladies	7
Othello	19	Otter	7
Morose	18	Bardolph	6
Trinculo	17	Catiline	6
Sir Politic	16	Cethegus	6
Prince Hal	15	Ghost (*Hamlet*)	6
Face	13	Pistol	6
Iago	12	Polonius	6
Caliban	11	Quickly	6
Cassio	11	Richard III	6
Cassius	11	Sycorax	6
Desdemona	10	Ananias	5
Macbeth	10	Cob	5
Sir Amorous La-Foole	10	Crispinus	5
Subtle	10	Dauphine	5
Volpone	10	Henry VIII	5
Ophelia	9	John of Wrotham	5
Rabbi Zeal-of-the-Land Busy	9	Juliet	5
Sylla's Ghost	9	Stephano	5
Truewit	9		

other leading character except Trinculo.[20] The new position of Hamlet is surprising only in that his popularity still falls so far short of Falstaff's. Since only about one-fourth of the references come before the Restoration, one is inclined to see in the Hamlet allusions as much Betterton as Shakespeare.

[20] See below, p. 126.

The most frequently named character of Jonson was Doll Common, and she ranks only fourth or eighth, depending on whether the Rymer allusions are counted or not. The marked difference between the relative popularity of Shakespeare's and Jonson's plays and their characters is most significant. In the play allusions, six creations of Jonson's (excluding the masques and poems) were more familiar than any of Shakespeare's; in character allusions Jonson ranks no higher than fourth or eighth. Again the evidence of the power of Shakespeare's characterization in spite of critical disapproval of the form of his plays is strikingly illustrated.

Why should Doll Common be more familiar than Face or Subtle or Sejanus, Volpone, Morose, or Rabbi Zeal-of-the-Land Busy? Two possible answers are suggested by the general character of the allusions to Doll. A number of them refer to her violence in the play, and several others use her name as a generic term for a prostitute. There is some implication here that Doll was more noteworthy on the stage than in the library, and a further suggestion that her name may have been a familiar one for a wanton before Jonson used it. I have found no such use antedating *The Alchemist*, however.

Considering the number of allusions to Brutus, it is not surprising that Caesar should be frequently named too, especially since the two are often mentioned together. Trinculo, on the other hand, seems a very minor character to be so familiar. Most of the references to him probably do not refer to the character Shakespeare created. A very few of them may refer to Trincalo in *Albumazar*. The popularity of this figure is indicated by Pepys's statement in his diary, February 22, 1667/68:

> To the Duke's playhouse, and there saw "Albumazar," an old play, this second time of acting. It is said to have been the ground of B. Jonson's "Alchymist;" but, saving the ridiculousnesse of Angell's part, which is called Trinkilo, I do not see anything extraordinary in it, but was indeed weary of it before it was done. The King here, and, indeed all of us, pretty merry at the mimique tricks of Trinkilo.

Obviously, Tomkis' character was popularly discussed in the 1660's after the revival of *Albumazar;* and, though every effort has been made here to separate allusions to

ALLUSIONS TO CHARACTERS, 1601–80

Falstaff	93	Bartholomew Cokes	5
Doll Common	13	Cethegus	5
Sir Politic	13	Collegiate Ladies	5
Morose	12	Desdemona	5
Hamlet	11	Juliet	5
Subtle	9	Macbeth	5
Face	8	Quickly-Hostess	5
Sylla's Ghost	8	Rabbi Zeal-of-the-Land Busy	5
Othello	7	Richard III	5
Prince Hal	7	Sir John Daw	5
Bardolph	6	Truewit	5
Brutus	6	Volpone	5
Sir Amorous La-Foole	6		

the *Tempest* Trinculo from those to the *Albumazar* Trincalo, a few passages might refer equally well to either, and some errors may have been made.

Even without the *Albumazar* confusion, the Trinculo of *The Tempest* most often referred to is probably Dryden and Davenant's elaborated character rather than Shakespeare's original. Again, the fact that about 90 per cent of the allusions occur after the Dryden-Davenant revision is suggestive. As in the case of the play allusions, it is illuminating to note how the allusions to characters are distributed when the last two decades of the century are excluded.

The figures for the first eight decades show not only that Trinculo had no particular vogue before the eighties but that, except for Falstaff, Jonson's major characters were much more popular than Shakespeare's before 1681, that is, there are 62 allusions to the ten Shakespearean characters in the list and 104 allusions to the fourteen Jonsonian characters [21] Again the evidence points to the fact that Shakespeare's reputation was largely a development of the last two decades of the century, and again the overwhelming popularity of Falstaff as Shakespeare's greatest creation is demonstrated.

To return to the list of all character allusions in the century, one is a bit puzzled at first glance by the vogue of Sir Politic Would-Be. The explanation is probably similar to that for Doll Common: the name came to be used as a generic one for pretenders to political knowledge.[22] As in the case of Doll Common, the aptness of the name may have been as influential as familiarity with the acting role.

The allusions to Prince Hal and those to Cassius are appendages to the reputations of Falstaff and Brutus. Most of the references to Prince Hal are found in Falstaff allusions; Hal is mentioned merely as the person Falstaff addressed or as his companion or the person whose questions elicited a famous reply. Cassius, similarly, is generally named in the Brutus allusions.

[21] These figures exclude all characters mentioned less than 5 times. When the allusions to these less popular characters are included, Jonson's characters are still more popular than Shakespeare's, though the ratio changes to about 22 to 17. These figures can be checked by adding the figures for the first eight decades in Classes 11 and 11a and subtracting the 93 Falstaff allusions from Shakespeare's total.

[22] See Vol. II, pp. 157, 184, and 229.

Of the other characters, only a few need comment or explanation. The Caliban allusions, like those to Trinculo, probably in most instances refer to the character in one of the revisions of *The Tempest* rather than in Shakespeare's original. I have found no references to the character before the Restoration. The same dictum applies to the Witches in *Macbeth* and to Sycorax and Stephano. The small number of allusions to characters from *Catiline* contrasts sharply with the popularity of the play.

Examining the list as a whole, one is at once struck with the obscurity of Shakespeare's heroines as compared with their vogue in the nineteenth and twentieth centuries. Only Desdemona and Ophelia seem to have made any impression worth mentioning. Lady Macbeth and Cleopatra, Beatrice, Portia, Rosalind, Miranda, Viola, Perdita, Imogen, and Cordelia are mentioned so seldom as to seem unknown. Clearly, the romantic comedies had very little appeal in the seventeenth century; and the same can be said with almost equal assurance of the romances, for the appeal of *The Tempest*—the only one with many allusions—lay in Dryden and Davenant's Trinculo and Caliban and their elaborate show, not in Shakespeare's play. The innocent heroine as Shakespeare conceived her had no charms for Caroline and Restoration audiences.

The ignoring of Lady Macbeth and Cleopatra, however, is not to be explained by their innocence. *Macbeth* in the version to which most references appear to be made had reduced the role of Lady Macbeth, while *Antony and Cleopatra* seems to have been seldom produced after the closing of the theaters, perhaps because it presented too many staging difficulties in the Restoration theater. Whatever the reasons for the situation, it is clear that the popularity of Shakespeare's characters in the seventeenth century is not due to the appeal of his heroines. They did not charm the writers of the seventeenth century as they have so many of the nineteenth and twentieth.

While Shakespeare received more recognition for his creation of character than for anything else, the characters which won him great acclaim were, first, Falstaff and then, far behind, the tragic heroes. There are more allusions to Falstaff than to Brutus, Hamlet, Othello, and Julius Caesar together, if we exclude, as we may reasonably do, the allusions in *A Short View of Tragedy*. Perhaps it is not surprising that the heroes of the romantic comedies—Orlando, Claudio, Bassanio, Antonio —are almost never mentioned, since modern readers find it difficult to believe that Shakespeare himself was very enthusiastic about them. More curious is the fact that men like Jacques, Touchstone, Benedick, Feste, and the Fool in *King Lear* seem no more familiar in the seventeenth century than the young lovers.

One cannot conclude, however, that only the astonishing vogue of Falstaff makes Shakespeare's seventeenth-century reputation as a creator of character greater than Jonson's. Even without the Falstaff allusions and even eliminating the characters generally mentioned with Falstaff—Prince Hal, Hotspur, Bardolph, Pistol, Mistress Quickly—the passages referring to Shakespeare's characters still outnumber those referring to Jonson's, 5 to 3. Clearly, the seventeenth-century writers thought that Shakespeare's one unquestioned superiority to Jonson was his characterization— and that his masterpiece was Falstaff.

CHAPTER VIII

CONCLUSIONS

After such a tedious analysis of thousands of allusions, what are we justified in concluding about the reputation which Shakespeare enjoyed in the seventeenth century? The question is not a fresh one, for various respected critics and scholars have declared themselves on the subject, often with notably slight reservations. Augustus Ralli said:

> The general average estimate of the century [1598–1694], however, was that Shakespeare was England's greatest, because most universal, poet—perhaps the world's greatest poet, because in drama he rivalled, if not surpassed, the Greek tragedians and the Latin comedians, and his stream of narrative verse flowed as smoothly as Ovid's. He is admitted to have excelled in "nature"—a word we should now replace by "realism": his readers or audience ascribing the tremendous impression on their minds from characters such as Hamlet, Lear, Macbeth to Shakespeare's literal rendering of external fact.[1]

Charles Knight asserted:

> Of the popularity of Shakspere in his own day the external evidence, such as it is, is more decisive than the testimony of any contemporary writer. He was at one and the same time the favourite of the people and of the Court.[2]

George Lyman Kittredge declared:

> In his own day, Shakspere was one of the best-known figures in England. He was held in high esteem, both as a man and as a poet, while in his capacity of dramatic author he was not only immensely popular, but was rated at something like his true value by most persons of taste and judgment.[3]

[1] *A History of Shakespearian Criticism* (2 vols.; Oxford, 1932), I, 10.

[2] *The Pictorial Edition of the Works of Shakspere* (1839–43), Suppl. Vol.: *A History of Opinion on the Writings of Shakspere*, p. 332.

[3] *Shakspere: An Address Delivered on April 23, 1916, in Sanders Theatre at the Request of the President and Fellows of Harvard College* (1916), p. 24.

These declarations on Shakespeare's reputation in his own time have been made by distinguished students of Shakespeare, men widely read in the literature of the seventeenth century. The assertions are evidently based on the tributes by well-known writers like Meres, Jonson, Harvey, Heminges, Condell, Milton, Hales, Benson, Digges, Margaret Cavendish, and Dryden. Yet the basis of these reputation estimates is obviously not broad enough; their authors have not considered the bulk of the statements about Shakespeare and his work in the seventeenth century, nor have they observed the precaution of comparing Shakespeare's reputation with the reputation of a contemporary dramatist of distinction like Jonson. The foregoing pages have demonstrated just how erroneous these three assertions are. Ralli's use of the comparisons with Greek and Latin drama and with Ovid is revealing, for such comparisons, though frequently used by the critics mentioned, are rare in the body of Shakespeare allusions taken as a whole. His statement about Shakespeare's rank as England's greatest dramatist is flatly contradicted by the allusion totals in Class 1. Even more misleading is his statement about the effect of the characters Hamlet, Lear, and Macbeth. These are modern, not seventeenth-century, favorites; in their own century their rank among the popular characters of Shakespeare and Jonson was seventh, eighty-seventh,[4] and seventeenth, respectively.

The statements by Knight and Kittredge are less specific than Ralli's, but the contention that Shake-

---

[4] Lear's rank cannot be given exactly, for twenty other characters of Shakespeare and Jonson are mentioned the same number of times as he is. Specifically, he ranks between eighty-sixth and one hundred and seventh.

speare was at "the same time the favourite of the people and the Court" is completely overthrown by the evidence of the allusions. Kittredge's "immensely popular" must at least be reduced to "second most popular," while Shakespeare's "true value" is scarcely indicated by the allusions in Classes 1, 2, 10, 12, and 15 or by the rank of his individual plays or even his individual characters.

So far as mere popularity is concerned, Jonson was evidently more popular in the seventeenth century than Shakespeare; for, when all allusions are judged by the same standard, 1,839 passages alluding to Jonson have been recorded, as compared to 1,430 to Shakespeare; and we can be sure that there are many more still unnoted allusions to Jonson than to Shakespeare. The many erroneous assertions that Shakespeare was the most popular dramatist of the century are derived from a reading confined to only the better-known critical passages or from a consideration of the indiscriminately swollen *Shakspere Allusion-Book* and the incomplete *Jonson Allusion-Book*.

This greater popularity of Jonson is not simply a matter of the grand totals of all allusions in the century. When the allusions are distributed chronologically, we find that he is referred to more frequently than Shakespeare in every decade of the century except the last. In the third and fourth decades there are twice as many allusions to Jonson as to Shakespeare; in the sixth and eighth decades Jonson's majority is slight; in the last decade Shakespeare's majority is only 7 in nearly 500. Various factors affecting these totals have been noted, but none of them alters the conclusion that steadily throughout the century until the last decade Jonson was more popular in England than Shakespeare.

But a dramatist's reputation is not to be judged by the numbers of references to him alone: some allusions are much more significant than others. Accordingly, the seventeenth-century allusions to Jonson and Shakespeare have been classified into twenty-two types and considered for the additional light they throw on the esteem in which the two men were held. Since many of the allusions contain several different types of statements, they are counted in more than one class, sometimes in as many as six or eight different classes. Therefore, the total number of allusions in the various classes greatly exceeds the 1,430 passages referring to Shakespeare plus the 1,839 passages referring to Jonson.

Perhaps the most significant class is the first one, made up of allusions in which the name of the dramatist is used alone as a standard of greatness. There are nearly three times as many such allusions to Jonson as to Shakespeare, more in every decade of the century—in the fourth, fifth, and sixth decades more than six times as many. A second class of allusions is made up of complete poems or long passages devoted to the poet. There are between three and four times as many such allusions to Jonson as to Shakespeare, more than four times as many in the first five decades of the century. Only in the third, ninth, and tenth decades are such allusions to Shakespeare more numerous, and in each of these three periods the numbers are small.

These two classes of allusions, because of their direct statement of popular esteem, are among the most revealing of all evidence concerning Shakespeare's reputation in the seventeenth century. The evidence is emphatic that only in the third, ninth, and tenth decades of the century did Shakespeare seriously rival Jonson's reputation as the great dramatist of England; and even in those three exceptional decades the combined total of allusions elevating Jonson is greater than the combined total of such allusions to Shakespeare.

There are four classes of allusions which consist of lists of English writers named in seventeenth-century histories, criticisms, or the like. Jonson is named in 322 such lists, Shakespeare in 271. Most of these inventories do not particularly distinguish the poets listed, but Jonson's name quite evidently occurred more frequently to such writers than Shakespeare's. Thus Jonson was the most widely remembered as well as the most frequently praised.

The next three classes of allusions are made up of quotations from the two poets, acknowledged and unacknowledged. Here the figures are less reliable than in the other classes because Shakespearean quotations are so much more widely recognized and reported than Jonsonian ones. Even so, 442 Jonsonian quotations in the works of seventeenth-century writers have been reported, 407 Shakespearean ones. It should be noted, however, that Jonson's lead is greatest in quotations simply assembled for their own sakes, particularly in commonplace books. Shakespeare leads in quotations used in context for their aptness or to bring to bear the weight of authority, especially in the last decade of the century. Evidently, at least by the end of the century, Shakespeare's unsurpassed ability to phrase effectively the popular truth was recognized. Jonson, as witness the commonplace books, throughout the century made the greatest appeal to the university student and the dilettante.

Allusions of Class 10 show that Jonson's plays are mentioned 767 times in the century to Shakespeare's 567—this in spite of the fact that there are about twice as many plays in the Shakespeare canon as in the Jonson. Not only was Jonson generally more admired and more familiar than Shakespeare, but Jonson's plays individually were more frequently discussed than Shakespeare's.

Only in the two classes of allusions referring to characters does Shakespeare's reputation approach the dominance which has been often asserted for him. His characters as literary creations or acting roles are referred to 733 times to Jonson's 329—a dominance all the more significant when compared to the relative number of allusions to the plays. Though the writers of the seventeenth century as a whole did not appreciate Shakespeare's unequaled genius, they evidently did see that he was the greatest creator of character among English dramatists.

Two classes of allusions are concerned with records of performances of the plays and masques of the two playwrights; nearly twice as many references to Jonson's productions were noted as compared to Shakespeare's. These allusions do not necessarily indicate that Jonson was performed more than Shakespeare in the century, but only that there was more discussion by literate persons of Jonsonian performances.

Allusions of Classes 14 and 15 are biographical but nonetheless significant evidence of reputation. Seventeen letters or copies of letters to Jonson in the seventeenth century have been thought significant and preserved; none of Shakespeare's has been so cherished. Similarly, there are 21 records of public honors conferred on Jonson or proposed for him; none for Shakespeare. These two groups of allusions, though small and significant chiefly for the first part of the century, seem to me eloquent of the great esteem which the century had for Jonson and of its comparative neglect of Shakespeare. Jonson was publicly and formally honored in his lifetime, and his relics were cherished after his death; Shakespeare enjoyed neither distinction.

Personal anecdotes and records of the two men make up Class 17, in which the Jonson allusions outnumber the Shakespeare ones about 3 to 2. But the evidence of Jonson's predominant reputation is greater than the figures suggest, for five-sevenths of the Shakespeare allusions of this class are business and legal records which would have been preserved for Shakespeare the man of property had he never written a line. The Jonson allusions are mostly personal anecdotes bearing witness to the impression made by the man's genius and his personality.

Two classes of allusions are composed of critical passages about the poets' work in general or about particular examples. Fifty-five such passages concern Shakespeare; 69 concern Jonson. Though the Jonson majority here is clear, it is misleadingly small. The reason is that such critical passages are not characteristic of the first half of the century when Jonson's dominance was greatest; before 1650 Jonson leads 15 to 8; after, only 54 to 47. Thus more critical attention was devoted in the century to Jonson than to Shakespeare, even though most such criticism was written after Shakespeare's reputation had begun to grow faster than Jonson's.

Finally, the miscellaneous passages alluding to the dramatists only incidentally and in none of the foregoing ways number 82 to Shakespeare and 138 to Jonson. Here again, though the writers show no particular interest in or knowledge of the two dramatists, the same preference for Jonson appears.

The totals in these various classes of allusions have indicated the general aspects of the two reputations fairly clearly, but further analysis was necessary to display the standing in the century of particular works and characters. Of the individual plays, the most frequently mentioned are all by Jonson—*Catiline*, *Volpone*, *The Alchemist*, *The Silent Woman*, *Sejanus*, and *Bartholomew Fair*. Each of these plays has more allusions in the century than any product of Shakespeare's pen. When ranked with Jonson's plays according to the number of seventeenth-century allusions, the modern favorites in the Shakespeare canon do not show up well. *Hamlet* is fifteenth, *Lear* thirty-sixth, *Othello* tenth, *Macbeth* eleventh, *As You Like It* sixty-eighth, *Twelfth Night* fiftieth, *The Merchant of Venice* sixtieth. Shakespeare's most frequently mentioned title is *The Tempest*, which ranks ninth, but an examination of the allusions shows that more than half of them probably refer to the Davenant-Dryden revision and not to Shakespeare's original. Next most popular are *Othello*, tenth; *Macbeth*, eleventh; and *Henry IV*, twelfth. The other histories and the comedies, particularly the romantic comedies, appear far down on the list.

Only in references to characters does Shakespeare hold a place anything like that which modern critics think rightfully his. Here the position of the two dramatists is the reverse of that in the play allusions. The seven most popular characters are Shakespeare's; and, though the characters from *Othello* are given an undue prominence by the elaborate discussion of the play in Rymer's *Short View of Tragedy*, even when the allusions from this analysis are omitted, five of the six most commonly mentioned characters are still Shakespeare's— Falstaff, Brutus, Hamlet, Julius Caesar, and Othello. Far and away the most popular is Falstaff, by all odds the most frequently mentioned play character of the century. He is mentioned three times as often as Brutus, five times as often as Hamlet, thirteen times as often as Macbeth, and six times as often as Jonson's most popular character, Doll Common. No other creation of Shakespeare's of any kind so captured the imaginations of seventeenth-century writers.

Altogether, the seventeenth-century allusions to Shakespeare and to Jonson when sifted and classified by the same standards give a reasonably clear picture of the comparative reputations of the two great dramatists between 1601 and 1700. Jonson's general popularity was greater than Shakespeare's from the beginning of the century to 1690; Shakespeare's reputation was growing more rapidly than Jonson's in the last two decades. Throughout the century Jonson was unchallenged in most critical writing as the greatest English dramatist, his popularity in critical writings being greater than his over-all popularity. This unchallenged rank is confirmed by the records of formal honors offered Jonson and the preservation of his relics—phenomena wholly absent in the records of Shakespeare. By and large, Jonson was quoted more often than Shakespeare, especially in gentlemen's commonplace books. Jonson's individual works were more widely known and praised than Shakespeare's, especially *Catiline*, *Volpone*, *The Alchemist*, *The Silent Woman*, and *Sejanus*. Performances of Jonson's plays and masques were discussed by literate people nearly twice as often as Shakespeare's. Shakespeare's greatest achievement was evidently thought to be his characters, and this aspect of his reputation alone clearly overshadowed Jonson's. Falstaff had no rival; but Brutus, Hamlet, and Othello also appear to be more widely known than any character of Jonson's.

All these comparisons, we must bear in mind, lead to an underestimation of Jonson's seventeenth-century reputation. The same standards have been applied here to the allusions to both poets, but in the search for allusions and records over nearly three centuries, the man-hours devoted to Shakespeare have exceeded by many times those devoted to Jonson. Hence, far more still unnoted Jonson allusions than Shakespeare allusions can be expected in the future, still further enhancing Jonson's reputation.

Clearly, Jonson, and not Shakespeare, was the dramatist of the seventeenth century. Only the modern enthusiasm for Shakespeare and the consequent overemphasis upon such seventeenth-century passages praising his works as have been frequently reprinted have blinded literary students to the obvious fact. Jonson himself could see that Shakespeare's plays are such

"as neither man nor Muse can praise too much," that
"he was not of an age, but for all time"; yet most of
Jonson's contemporaries had not so much understanding. Jonson, whose plays best exemplified the accepted
critical dogma of the time and who most vigorously
preached the dogma, could perceive the genius of the
artist who defied the rules. But for lesser minds the
"learned Jonson" was the man.

INDEX

⟦PRINTED IN U·S·A⟧